G000127596

Fiv
Hot...
Five Minutes
Cold...
A TEACHER'S HUMOROUS MEMORIES

BY

PETER FOSTER

Grosvenor House
Publishing Limited

The right of Peter Foster to be identified as the author of this
work has been asserted in accordance with Section 78
of the Copyright, Designs and Patents Act 1988

The book cover picture is copyright to Peter Foster

This book is published by
Grosvenor House Publishing Ltd
28-30 High Street, Guildford, Surrey, GU1 3EL.
www.grosvenorhousepublishing.co.uk

Any real names in this book have been used with
the permission of the person concerned

A CIP record for this book
is available from the British Library

ISBN 978-1-78148-407-4

Contents

For all my school friends

A big thank you to Alex Lange for the cartoons

Drawings by Peter Foster

Introduction

Why become a teacher? Well, at eighteen I didn't really know what to do with myself. Academically I was lazy, although I had managed to pick up a fair number of exam passes. My one vague idea of becoming a vet was linked more to many enjoyable hours with the family guinea pigs and mice than any particular vocational gift or drive ... I even failed biology 'O' level the first time round!

I was, however, quite good at sport; school captain at football and basketball and reasonable at racket sports, so my dad and I sat down one evening and despite interruptions for food and *Morecambe and Wise*, came up with the idea that I would apply to some teacher training colleges as a good 'let's have more sport and delay the career decision' option, with P.E. as the obvious subject area; and thus I embarked upon a series of applications, visiting some colleges where brutal tests were applied, most of which I surprisingly passed.

Unfortunately, some institutions only accepted the 'Superman' type of international athlete that I clearly wasn't, whilst others were not in a particularly exciting place, or just too near home!

Yes, I had developed the wanderlust of youth! Six foot two inches of raw power itching to leave home and be unleashed on an unsuspecting world! By a strange quirk of fate my destination was to be decided during the men's singles final at Wimbledon...

No, I wasn't playing that year, but it was in the Centre Court spectator area that my mum and I met Cora, a delightful lady from Belfast.

It so happened that amongst six or seven recent college applications I had sent off, one was for Stranmillis College, Belfast.

In the moments between games and sets we started talking about Northern Ireland and she kindly offered to put me up should I get an interview. Well I did...I liked the brand new college ... they liked me ... it was a long way from home, and I was treated like a lord for a weekend by Cora and her family.

Thus started three great years in Ireland, north and south, but more of that later, to be sure!

It was the start of a career in teaching that lasted thirty-eight years. My memories include rewarding and difficult periods, but always the changing situations that are peculiar to schools.

The clearest memories are the funny incidents whether accidental or planned, and it is these that will tend to fill up quite a few of the following pages. I will also never forget the great teachers and other staff I have worked with, and of course the many pupils who have made me laugh and kept me young inside.

Oh, the title? ... Well if you bring a football class in late and it is necessary to get them off quickly to the next lesson, the showering process can be speeded up dramatically by the threat of cold water after the first five minutes for the 'slow coaches'. A casual procession intent on avoiding as much of double maths as possible is suddenly transformed into an Australian sheep dip!

A short history of Ireland

This is not primarily a book about me, but rather the experiences I have had in a number of schools. It would, however, be wrong not to mention my college years in Ireland, as this was the place where I discovered that I liked teaching, learnt so much, made some great friends, and fell in love with both the country and its people.

It wasn't, literally, the greatest start to my teaching career, however, as my Austin A30 refused to budge in south east London on the September morning I was leaving home. I had spent many hours shining it up and even hand-painted the outside in bright colours, but I had never been able to solve the reoccurring flat battery problem. Thus, the poignant, tearful farewell between my parents and I was spoiled somewhat as they were forced to push-start me on my way to Liverpool for the ferry to Belfast the next day.

As I drove through London towards the M1, my spirits were further dampened by the driving rain and heavy traffic and I must admit to one or two doubts about the wisdom of leaving home at such a tender age (eighteen)! But, by the time I had reached a surprisingly clean service station on the motorway and eaten a full English breakfast, I had recovered my sense of independence and adventure. I did, however, forget to park 'the Beast' on a slope, but on this occasion it grudgingly agreed to start. Apart from a nasty jam at the interchange between the M1 and M6 the rest of the journey was fairly uneventful, and even the weather improved as the sounds of the sixties on my radio carried me onwards towards the Irish Sea.

I must have still been feeling a little vulnerable by the time I reached Liverpool, as instead of heading for The Cavern or other places of interest and fun, I merely downed a packet of fish and chips, checked where the ferry terminal was, and then hit the sack ready for the early rise required to catch the boat.

The fry-up provided at my bed and breakfast was so substantial that I made a mental note about the healthy diet required for a P.E. student, before bump-starting the way to my future. The ferry crossing was going to be about seven hours and I was actually looking forward to some invigorating strolls on the deck and some friendly conversation in the bar and restaurant. Who knows, I might even meet a fellow first year student at Stranmillis? The reality was that the crossing was so rough that I felt sick for a good part of the way.

Believing fresh air to be the cure, I spent the third hour on deck, but the boat was lurching sideways (as was I) and this only made my stomach feel worse. So I made the fatal mistake of heading for the bar which was full of hundreds of Manchester United fans who were celebrating a thumping home victory against Arsenal the previous afternoon, as well as singing the praises of their own Northern Ireland hero, George Best (who was to come back to haunt me in a few weeks

time). An hour or so later, I was throwing up on deck after a few too many pints with 'the lads'.

My entrance into Northern Ireland was, again, far from glorious, as my car was one of the first off and was holding everyone up as it failed to start yet again! It chugged into action after a few crew members set me off and I managed to find my way to my digs by early evening. The landlady was very friendly and insisted that I had something to eat and I must admit I did have a very empty stomach! There were two other students staying in the house and I got to know them and parts of Belfast quite well in the few days I had before term started.

My impressions of the college had already been gained at the interview and a more detailed tour on my first day confirmed that it was spanking new with very good sports facilities and lots of good-looking women floating around...The omens were good! This feeling was further enhanced when I met my fellow first year students who were all from Northern Ireland and had a range of sporting abilities, with rugby being the most noticeable. I quickly made friends with Billy from Clogher, who was to become a close friend and guide to all things Irish for the next three years. I was one of only eight English students in the college.

I quickly settled into a routine of sport and study by day and fun at Stranmillis or in Belfast in the evening and at weekends. Such was the hospitality of the Irish that I was constantly being invited to all parts of Northern Ireland at the weekends and my eyes were opened to the beauty of Antrim, Donegal and the Mourne Mountains, to name just a few places on any-one's 'must visit' list. Belfast also proved to be a surprise as at first glance it seemed a run-down relic of the Industrial Revolution, but I soon became acquainted with some great pubs and clubs and there were also regular social events such as dances at Queen's University. Life was very good and I managed to make the first team at basketball and soccer, which was not only a good level but did wonders for my own ability and progress. In my contact home I was able to report that I was enjoying college life very much.

But the day of reckoning was fast approaching! I had to go on my first teaching practice and I hadn't a clue if I was going to be any good, or enjoy the experience.
I didn't think too much about it at the time, but I realise now that we were receiving some great lectures and practical sessions on P.E. and geography (my second subject), but no one was providing us with any advice about class management, lesson planning and discipline. I approached one of the senior P.E. lecturers with this concern to be met with the response, 'Don't worry about that Peter! Sure, you've either got it or you haven't.' This was hardly reassuring and the realisation that I had committed myself to becoming a teacher was beginning to be a concern in my otherwise idyllic existence of sport and fun. My nerves were further jangled when I discovered that my first posting was to teach football at a large school just outside the city that had a famous former pupil; guess who ...George Best.

The night before my first teaching practice was one of troubled sleep and dreams, with George Best repeatedly dribbling past me and scoring the vital final goal for United. As my teammates glared at me for missing yet another tackle, their faces gradually changed into laughing teenage boys, until I eventually curled up on the ground and sobbed.

Far from refreshed, I set out the next morning with a fellow P.E. student on the back of his motorbike. I was nearly saved from the ordeal of facing my first class by my nervousness and inexperience on this machine. The road to school was fast and contained some quite long bends, which the passenger would normally be required to lean into. I didn't feel comfortable with this and repeatedly risked disaster by leaning in the opposite direction as 'upright' felt safer. After a couple of stops and requests to save our lives, I managed to adjust my lean and we arrived safely, but it was agreed that the attempt to save petrol should be ended and I was to travel in my car in the future.

We signed in at the secretaries' office and went our separate ways agreeing to meet up to compare notes at lunch. While I was waiting to meet the head of P.E. my spirits were lifted by a glance at the school notice-board, which announced that shepherd's pie followed by sponge pudding was on the menu for lunch. The secretary asked me to go to meet the head of P.E. in the gym as he was quite busy and a not too threatening twelve-year-old boy was assigned to escort me. As we walked through the school George Best was staring at me from numerous photographs which seemed to increase in number in the final corridor before the gym. The boy asked me to wait outside for a moment and then went in to find the teacher. I turned my head to yet another photo and felt sure that George's smile was not only sarcastic, but aimed at me.

At that moment the boy rushed out of the gym and off down the corridor. George's smile was even broader

... I waited a few seconds and then decided to go in. In the middle of the gym was a teacher with a headlock on a boy I judged to be about fifteen. The lad was quite strong and despite being 'strangled' by a sixteen-stone rugby player, managed to break free and proceeded to shout some expletives at the teacher before leaping at him. The teacher expertly caught him on his back and proceeded to throw him to the ground in a move that would not have been out of place on the telly during the regular Saturday afternoon *Grandstand* wrestling slot. The boy was winded but unhurt and after a few more expletives decided that retreat was the wisest course when faced with 'Giant Haystacks'.

The head of P.E. rearranged his clothing, stretched his neck a bit and then with a beaming smile approached me and after telling me his name, said, 'Hallo, you must be Peter ... welcome to the school. Sorry about that bit of crack, but don't worry, the kids are not all like him!' He then told me that my first class would be here in five minutes and that he was off to the staff-room. If I had any problems I was to send Sean (a good lad) to get him.

Before I had too much time to analyse this dramatic start to my teaching career the class arrived and to my surprise they headed for the changing rooms with hardly a glance in my direction (they loved their football).

I had prepared the lesson well but felt very nervous as I gave the first instructions to the lads. My attempt to demonstrate how to keep the ball up with a combination of knee and foot started badly with a duff 'flick up' and there were a few sniggers from the audience, but to my relief the second attempt succeeded and it resulted in a reasonable demonstration. I told the lads to attempt this with mixed results, but they were at least trying. I glanced at my notes and realised that in my anxiety I had forgotten the warm-up run and stretching, but was feeling slightly more relaxed and no one had attacked me yet. I resisted the inevitable request of 'when are we going to have a game?' and moved into some dribbling and passing before rewarding the group with some five-a-side for the last ten minutes.

I got to know some of the class as they changed at the end of the lesson and a few seemed impressed that I had come all the way from London to learn how to teach. The final comment as the pupils left was from the undoubted star of the group. After asking if it was my first lesson he pronounced, 'Well, that wasn't too bad for your first lesson, but you're no George Best!'

I felt exhausted at the end of that first day and didn't even try to keep up with the rugby lads' drinking in the college bar that evening, but as I settled down to sleep at a very early 10.30p.m. I felt a quiet satisfaction and pleasure as I realised I had survived and even enjoyed this first day ... and the sponge pudding was excellent!

Despite the dramatic start, the school proved to be a good one with some very enthusiastic and talented sportsmen and very helpful teachers. I also volunteered to take a geography class to cover a teacher's absence (saving the school some cover teacher money) which I thought might give me some good brownie points with the geography department and the headmaster. By the end of my three-week stint I realised that, more by luck than judgement, I had found a future career!

I would love to fill some more pages in praise of Stranmillis and Ireland, but I will control myself and just end this section with a few examples of the practical jokes that my fellow P.E. students loved to play on their gullible English visitor.

Rugby in Dublin

I loved watching rugby and regularly went down to Dublin with a few of the lads to watch the Irish team's home games, with the understanding that if England were playing and won I would be in for some sort of punishment. 'We won't kill you though, as we need you to drive us back to Belfast,' was a reassurance from Billy.

On the first occasion, luckily, Australia were the visitors and expected to thrash the Irish. Ireland did lose but only just and that Saturday evening the mood was good as we downed a few drinks at one of the best bars in the city. At closing time I had the thought that we had nowhere to stay, but with a wink Danny announced that he knew some girls at university in Dublin and had arranged for us to 'crash' at their digs. And so the party carried on into the early hours of Sunday morning.

I have never been a good drinker (although in the first weeks of my starting college I did try to prove I was a 'big boy' by downing as many Guinnesses as possible before throwing up) and on this occasion I had way too many and didn't surface till about midday on Sunday. Most of the lads seemed to have gone out for fresh air, although Billy was still fast asleep in the bath.

I stumbled to the window and looked out on a beautiful Dublin morning. Some birds were singing, the Liffey was sparkling in the morning sun (we were upwind so didn't get the smell) and a number of cheery voices were to be heard in the street below ... but my car was gone!

I looked up and down the road a few times in case a hangover had affected my memory of the exact parking position... it had gone. I shouted something or other as I stood up quickly and then shouted something else as my head banged against the top window. This was enough to momentarily stir the occupants of the room, but after a few curses and mumbles they all settled down to sleep again, except Billy who was approaching me with a bit of a wobble. I quickly explained that the car was missing; he had a look and told me that it was quite common for a car with out of town number plates to go missing in Dublin. I got quite angry, but eventually realised that this is probably what had happened. I began to worry because there was an important pre-exam lecture on Monday morning back at Stranmillis and we really didn't have much time to sort out the car before setting off back to Belfast.

One of the girls had been woken by all this commotion and promised to report the theft to the police 'if you would just shut it and let me get some sleep!' Billy agreed to this and suggested that we thumb a lift back as we had no money left. The same girl (desperate for peace) threw some money across the room which was our bus fare out of town to the road north, and Billy told me that the other lads had taken off to meet some friends in the night when I had gone to sleep and that they would make their own way back if they hadn't returned by the morning.

So it was that an hour or so later we were in the rear of an open-back van, in pouring rain, on our way back to the north, courtesy of a kind farmer who had some livestock to collect from a farm just south of Belfast.

My foul mood wasn't improved by Billy who thought the whole episode quite funny, with little thought for my beloved car or the pneumonia we were likely to contract. In addition the driver loved to sing and requested that we joined in the choruses of a series of Irish favourites. I was not in the mood but Billy was quite happy to join in, especially as he could see that this was winding me up even more!

We were nearing the border when they both started up with 'Wild Rover'. The jaunty nature of this ditty was the last straw, especially as Billy was digging me in the ribs in an effort to make me join in and I was just about to ask the driver to stop singing when a familiar vehicle came into site at the side of the road. At first I couldn't believe it, but sure enough it was the Beast and joy of joys, the door was open, keys in the ignition and it seemed to be in one piece. A quick check confirmed that there was no damage inside or out and I was about to break into song when I noticed Billy pointing stern-faced at a piece of paper on the screen. It read, 'Next time could you at least leave enough petrol in the tank! And you need to fix the starter motor, we had to push twice!'

Billy burst out into laughter and the farmer sounded his horn, anxious to get started again. I turned the key and the battery was flat. I turned it again and it spluttered for a few moments before giving in to the fact that there was indeed no petrol.

I was sure that this was the work of 'the lads', but Billy tried to calm me down by pointing out that it could have been any one of thousands returning north after the game. The hooter went again and I crouched, head in hands, not being sure what to do or who to vent my anger on when I received a tap on the shoulder. Expecting a sarcastic comment from Billy I was about to let rip verbally when I realised it was a stranger with a smiling face, who volunteered to look after my car until I could get back to fix it. His house was just nearby and he would also help us push it over to the drive.

By now I had had enough. I was not a member of the AA or any Irish equivalent. The horn had sounded again, it was still raining and we needed to get back for a lecture, preferably before dark. I gratefully accepted the kind gentleman's offer, gave him my phone number and promised to be back as soon as possible. As I climbed into the wet van, I wished I was tucked up in bed with my favourite teddy bear and a hot water bottle.

I never did find out whether the car was stolen or borrowed, but my suspicions were aroused by a number of anonymous letters I received the following week containing useful information and contact numbers with regard to car security ...It was, however, a comment from Brian 'Doddy' Dawson (one of my fellow P.E. students) which finally made me laugh and 'move on' ...'Peter, I hope you're going to get the car soon. We wouldn't be wanting to pay a train fare to get to the next game in Dublin!'

Birthday celebrations

It was my twenty-first birthday and I was a long way from home. I didn't have enough money to fly to London, which was quite handy as most of my friends were now at college with me and the P.E. boys had promised a great night out involving women, dancing and drink ... I was also excited at the prospect that the venue was a surprise.

I was blindfolded and led out to a car by 'Fitz' who assured me I was going to love the evening. The drive was about twenty minutes, as I was able to judge the time by the fact that ten songs had passed on the very loud radio, including quite a few golden oldies from the sixties that were inevitably the standard two minutes long. I was led into a place that sounded a little quiet for a club and told to sit down on a chair and wait for the surprise. I had to promise not to take off the blindfold. I heard a door close and then some muffled conversations from the other side. Not wanting to spoil the fun, or anger some rather hefty rugby players, I contented myself with thoughts of the fun evening to follow. About five minutes passed with nothing happening, so I decided to sneak a view of my surroundings. But just as I was about to move the blindfold down an inch or two Billy opened the door and shouted, 'Don't be moving now Peter, we're almost ready!' Another five minutes of relative silence followed, so I once again decided to take a sneaky peek, fully expecting a crowd to shout out 'Happy Birthday'.

A dirty wall appeared just a few feet in front of me. To the sides were a pair of even dirtier walls, one containing a toilet roll holder with a message on the paper, 'Would you hurry up in that toilet. Sure, you'll stink and the club closes at midnight!'

I came out of the loo looking for blood, especially as 'the lads' in the car were wetting themselves with laughter. As I approached them I issued some uncharacteristic threats, at which point they drove off about

100 yards. As Billy waved me towards the car I almost saw the funny side of things so I ambled forward slowly, not wishing to show I had completely lost my cool. Danny (the driver) smiled and as my hand moved towards the door handle the car shot off again! I was in a real sulk now and started to walk off in the other direction. The car reversed ahead of me and I heard some laughter being stifled by Billy. I had no intention of trying the door again and walked determinedly past. When I was a safe distance away, Billy stepped out and said, 'Sure Peter, we can't let you back in while you're in such a foul temper … come on, I promise we'll give you a great time from now on.'

The options were as follows. I was somewhere in Belfast with no prospect of fun if I sulked off, or I could take the risk that the lads would eventually have pity on me and I would have a proper twenty-first … There were only a few hours left of my twentieth year and as I looked at Billy he held out his hands as if to embrace me. The jokes were over and the real business of the evening was about to start! I walked back to the car and Billy opened the door. I looked at everyone's faces, they all looked sincere and then noticing the seat was vacant slid in quickly only to land on a whoopee cushion expertly and quickly placed by Merv … cue more laughter!

It was only a few minutes to the club and as I gingerly entered the premises who should be there, but the Dublin girls! It was starting to feel like a twenty-first at last! And wasn't that the best-looking of the girls handing me a beer and saying how much she had been looking forward to seeing me again …all right!

After a few beers and a lot of attention from the girls I was on cloud nine, especially as my 'friends' seemed to be concerned with their own drinking and womanising by now. Billy and his girl raised a glass to me from the other side of the room and I felt a slight tinge of guilt for ever doubting their good intentions.

Sinead asked me if I was going to sing in the upcoming karaoke session (actually, I'm not sure if that was what it was called back in those days) and as she held me close in a smoochy dance, how could I refuse?

She told me how Billy had told her that I did a great version of 'Wild Rover', which should have been a danger signal, but as my drinks had been 'adjusted' from the moment we entered the club my already dubious powers of common sense had deteriorated even further and I found myself singing this Irish classic to rapturous (rigged) applause. I was so intoxicated by this unexpected approval of my singing that I asked for any requests... 'Danny Boy' was quickly shouted out and I sang this poignant ditty to a silent, mesmerised audience. I even noticed Sinead wiping a tear away on the last verse. How Billy had convinced a room of maybe a hundred or more people to go along with this wind-up and react as if I was Elvis is beyond me . . . but I was the centre of attention and loving it!

We waved the girls off in their car back to Dublin at about 6a.m. and I thought that was the end of a (finally) great twenty-first. But as we rolled along in the car singing more Irish classics, Billy leaned over and said, 'Pete, have you had a good evening?' The generous hug and happy mumble he received from me was a clear 'yes' to this question and so he added, 'Well there's one more surprise, but you have to be blindfolded again ... I swear you won't end up in a toilet!' I had no idea about what day it was by this stage, but still asked for reassurance from the others that it was a 'good' surprise, when Danny (the most innocent-looking of the group) replied, 'Peter, you've been a real sport today with all the tricks we've played on you, we all want to do something really special to finish off the evening.'

A few minutes later I was led blindfolded across what seemed to be a fairly quiet open area with some shingle-like surface beneath my feet. A beach party was my first thought and I even imagined that when the blindfold was removed, the Dublin girls would miraculously reappear, dancing on the sand resplendent in Hawaiian beachwear. It was then that I passed out.

I was roused by some sharpish pains in my arms; aching, stiff legs, and the sound of talking, no laughter, in the distance. I vaguely realised that I was bound to some sort of post, before another sensation, the need to go to the loo, kicked in quite rapidly. I couldn't see anything and I was beginning to develop a thumping headache. Panic started to creep in to my mind as I began to remember the events of the previous night. Where was I, and why was I tied up? I feebly shouted out 'Billy' a couple of times, but no one came to my assistance. A second later I could feel my blindfold being removed and my senses quickened as I realised my situation.

I was in the centre of the college's hard surface playing area, tied to one of the goal posts. In front of me were hundreds of students and lecturers on their way to the first lectures of the day. To my left was the college canteen, where I could see bodies rocking back and forth and a few pointing at me. Some spontaneous applause began on the pathway in front of me as I felt myself being roughly released from my bonds. I had accidently kicked over a large piece of cardboard which had been by my feet and on picking it up was greeted with the words, 'Twenty-one today, do not disturb'. As I turned to see my saviour I was further horrified to find that it was the chief P.E. lecturer, who without a glimmer of a smile or word of sympathy pronounced, 'Happy Birthday Peter. By my reckoning you have thirty minutes to take a shower and be ready for my lecture.' There was also an over strong slap on the back as he strode off.

I am not sure how I got through the next few days of humiliation and wisecracks, but I did at least achieve a sort of celebrity status as the Englishman who was incredibly green and gullible and couldn't take his drink!!

I will never forget Ireland and the generosity I received from so many people. Despite the resurgence of 'the Troubles' during my three years in Belfast, I was torn between staying there or returning to London for my probationary year. In the end it was the offer of a flat share with my best friend that took me back over the water.

Billy said he was going to Australia, Dorothy married and went to Canada, Liz moved to Bromley and surprised me by turning up at a parents' evening with her daughter at the school where I was working, and Danny said he was going 'abroad' ...but with regard to Louise, Brian, Anne and so many others, I haven't a clue where they are and what sort of life they have had ... but I wish them all well.

Visitors from afar

How many of you are experiencing one or more of the following? You're fed up with work, your family are a pain in the neck, the country is drifting into ruin and the government doesn't seem to see the desperate situation you're in? Teachers often feel like this, a state of mind further influenced by the situation in their school. Too much marking, not enough money, disruptive kids and a never-ending stream of initiatives from the new Education Secretary, to mention just a few of the regular contenders in the 'moan stakes'. The cure? A visitor from abroad, with a willingness to learn and a sense of wonder at a new environment and culture.

One particular boy in my class a few years ago was Akira, whose family were in Britain for a year as his dad had a contract with a London firm. I had grown to expect hard work and excellent behaviour from Japanese pupils but he and his father added a new dimension. Whenever I made a request for information in the standard pupil contact book I started to receive quite detailed replies from Mr Iwama, showing not only his pleasure at Akira's rapid progress, but also an account of the families latest 'adventures' in England and beyond. These charming 'letters' made me realise the good things around us, how fortunate we are to be living in this country, and also the simple pleasures that we take for granted, or grow out of noticing quite so much. They made me think twice before I started to moan about my school or country!

I hope the following selections capture the humour and insight of these letters and I wish Akira and his family well in Japan and thank them for allowing me to reproduce the following.

9th Sept.

After summer holiday Akira got a little taller and much heavier. I cannot push him down any more in the Japanese style wrestling (Sumo).

But his English is not good enough yet, especially to understand the text of English. I always chase him with the text book whenever I have got some time. The other day I succeeded in catching him and I let him read the poem in the text which he was taught that day.

As he arrived at the verse 'who threw words like stones', he was much moved and said 'What a terrific poem it is! I never realized it says such a touching thing! I wish I had not dreamed at the lesson.'

K. Iwama

Akira was 'moved' because he had experienced some bullying from one or two pupils. His father was very calm about the situation and through this simple poem and the family's good sense, he soon learnt how to handle verbal bullying to such an extent that one of the culprits not only apologised but became one of Akira's best friends.

27th Nov.
It was a few weeks ago. I did not feel like going to Paris as I thought of the trouble of language and the balance of the bank. But Akira was quite keen on going there. I was persuaded by his eagerness. He seemed to be going to try his French.

He enjoyed some vehicles – British railway, Sealink boat, French railway, L'autobus and Metro. He enjoyed the Tour Eiffel, Chateau Versailles as well as French dishes.

On the way back I asked him what French words he had used. He said to me, 'Only three' – 'Ou est la lavabo?', 'C'est combien?' and 'Je voudrais ici'.

What a useful language his French was!
K.Iwama

Shortly before Christmas I wrote home that Akira had made a beautiful model boat for a history lesson.

10th Dec.
Thank you, Mr Foster.
I have a story about the boat. During last weekend Akira grappled with the homework of history lesson. He is fond of it and much fonder of such a homework. I helped him in collecting some materials and giving some advice and we went to Greenwich Maritime

museum and bought some picture cards of 'galleon'. He was a little too ambitious in his model making and after many hours he became tired. The last and most important process was to build the masts up. I advised him to take a break until the next day and he left for bed a little depressed at the size of his work still to do. To my astonishment, I found Akira, very early in the morning, trying to build the masts up carefully and it looked very good! The parent's advice used to be given no heed by their children. To be honest, I didn't expect it this time either, but actually Akira took my words seriously.

The Christmas present to Akira must become better than what was thought of before.

Thank you again, Mr Foster.

Have a nice Christmas!

K. Iwama

2nd Feb.

About four o'clock it began to snow. It was lying when I left London. On the way the spark brightened the black twigs with snow on both sides of the railway. It was nearing about ten, but people were enjoying the snow.

When I arrived in my house it seemed quiet. Opening door, Akira and his sister showed me. They amazed at the snow, 'snow! snow!'

They led me to the back room. Akira opened the curtain. There appeared a snow man! They'd been enjoying the snow too.

As soon as I opened the package of fish and chips they vanished immediately. I realised snow made appetite.

Snow is a gift given by nature. It purifies everything. English snow makes people happy besides.

K. Iwama

15th March

Akira waved a sheet of paper proudly before my eyes. It was a French test paper at whose bottom some words were written '100%, excellent'. It was a test on the conjugation of some 'er' verbs. I reminded I was so much troubled with 'aimer' that I almost stopped 'aimering' itself when I learnt French many years ago.

I asked him how he learnt them by heart and why he became suddenly clever.

He did not reply it directly but just told me that he found that French differs from English and French verbs vary according to each person and each number and that he learnt them by heart just looking at a list on the board which was written by the French teacher.

I praised and encouraged him but never made the slightest mention that there are different types of verb, a lot of irregular verbs, imperfect subjunctive and so on.

He is still too young to be troubled with these things and also love, but I hope that he will be energetic enough to master them both in time.

K. Iwama

5th May

Every weekend we go to museums to spend our last days as significantly as possible.

Natural History Museum is one of Akira's most favourite ones. We went there several times already. Imperial War Museum, National Maritime Museum are also his favourites.

Last week and the week before we went to Victoria and Albert Museum. What a vast museum! We only saw about half of it. But what an interesting museum it is!

Akira has been fascinated by it. Although his mother and I were a little bit exhausted, he is insisting to go there again to see the rest. We have been persuaded by his avarice curiosity.

On reflection, I find that Akira's desire to look at things – museums, castles, houses, gardens, natural beauties and something like that, has been our driving force to travel about this country.

K.Iwama

Of course, not everyone who comes to this country is as lucky as Akira.

It is difficult to imagine how one pupil must have felt when he arrived in the 1990s from war-torn Somalia. His mother, father and brother had all been killed in the conflict and he had been found, barely alive, after hiding in the wild for many months. After passing through a number of organisations in Africa who managed to help him back to reasonable physical health, John (not his real name) eventually arrived in south London in the care of a family and a placement at our school. I happened to be his head of year and I must say I was very worried about how he would adapt after experiencing such terrible events and also because he could speak very little English.

Inevitably, one or two of the less intelligent pupils gave John a bit of a hard time about his lack of English and quiet nature, but in general the boys and girls at school made him feel welcome and a few also started to spend time with him in and out of school. We often underestimate young peoples' understanding and intelligence in these situations and it was heart-warming to witness how some difficult situations were dealt with, not by a teacher or a system, but by a caring fellow pupil. In a few weeks he had a nice group of friends and was beginning to show signs of coping with his past. The pastoral care system was also instrumental in helping John during this difficult time in his life and the special needs department deserved a medal for their support and tuition.

Within a few months John had settled down so well that he had been given the nickname 'Smiler'. His English had improved to such an extent that he was able to take part quite actively in some lessons. He also loved watching American sitcoms and action films at home and he had learnt some phrases from these which he loved to 'show off' to me as we passed during the school day. Thus I would be greeted every morning with 'Yo Mr Foster, how they hanging, Dude?' and if he hit a home run at baseball it would be 'I'm the man, high fives Mr Fos!'. These and other cheeky quips increased his 'street cred' with the other pupils so much that years later he would still use them, pretending he didn't completely understand the meaning of the words, even though his English had become quite good.

The fact that John enjoyed sport really helped him in his early weeks at school. His whole demeanour would change as he got ready for some sporting action, especially as he was quite good at athletics and had reasonable hand-eye coordination.

When he arrived at school, there was some debate about which year he should be placed in as there were no records of either his birth place or date. On the physical side he seemed to be about fourteen, but he informed us that he thought he was twelve and the decision was taken to place him in year seven as his basic English was so poor. He certainly stood out in the classroom, being a good few inches taller than not only everyone in his year group, but also most of year eight! This was, however, undoubtedly the best arrangement for his academic progress and he seemed to get on well with the boys and girls in the year as well as a few older pupils.

The doubts about his age proved a bonus for the P.E. department as we were able to enter John in a number of sports where his extra size and strength produced excellent results. I must say I did feel a slight twinge of guilt as he rose above the opposition defence to head the winning goal in the second round of the local football cup and their players did seem to pass the ball quite quickly when the better option seemed to be to take John 'on' in a one-to-one situation!

It was in athletics that he really starred. He won the district shot put with an effort that was not particularly noticeable from a technical point of view, but owed a great deal to the fact that it was released from a considerable height and with a great deal of force. The high jump was also won with a rather amateurish scissor kick, which succeeded due to a powerful spring and a much higher centre of gravity than all the other competitors. After this event I started to receive some curious glances from one or two of the other competing schools' sports teachers and eventually a couple came over to have a chat with me, but gracefully accepted that we had no proof of John's real age and were acting on the best information available. I also gave some of them a brief outline of his background and perhaps they kindly decided that he needed some 'success' in his life.

The final event of the afternoon was the 1,500 metres. This was John's last event as competitors were limited to three, unfortunately. (In one inter – school match without these restrictions, John had won all the events with the exception of one or two that had been running at the same time for his age group.)

As the competitors lined up I could sense the despair of John's fellow runners as they stared up at the 'Goliath' they were expected to compete against. John decided to give them all about 20 metres start and responded to my frantic waving him forward with a smiling 'No problemo Mr Fos!' (Arnold Schwarzenegger in *Terminator?*), and had promptly caught everyone up by the end of the first lap. The race was so easy that he slowed down and waved everyone back towards him on at least two further occasions, giving me a thumbs-up each time as reassurance, but it was on the last lap that I nearly had a heart attack! For some reason, John had sprinted well ahead of everyone just before the end of the penultimate lap. I thought he had miscounted and waved him forwards. To my relief he carried on, but it was in the back straight that his intentions became evident. A friend of his who was also in the school team had been told to wait there by John with a bottle of water. John stopped, took some casual gulps and then proceeded to chat to his friend, seemingly oblivious of the rest of the field who willingly passed him with new enthusiasm. Knowing that to take a drink from another was actually against the rules for this event, my head was firmly planted between both hands. Suddenly some cheering from some of our pupils caused me to glance out between my fingers, to see John starting off again just in time to overtake the field to win in what was actually an excitingly close finish. He even had time to stare across at the second place runner with about 30 metres to go and give him a big smile and shake of the head.

Of course I knew that disqualification loomed and thought that the smiling face of the track judge who approached me reflected the fact that the second-placed runner, who was from his school, was about to be promoted to first. Much to my surprise the judges had decided to let the result stand and he had come to tell me that they hadn't had such a good laugh for a long time. John hugged the teacher enthusiastically before setting off on a victory lap, at the end of which he apologised to me with a touching 'I made your day, Mr Fos!' (*Dirty Harry*).

Although John's circumstances in life were rather extreme, his story is, nevertherless, a reminder of the power of sport in transforming young people's lives. He became a bit of a celebrity with the other students and not only managed to survive, but prosper in a strange society which he has now made his new home and workplace. At the prize-giving ceremony at the end of his first year I must admit to having a lump in my throat as John beamed a smile at me from the school stage after receiving the year seven sports prize from a slightly bemused (and much smaller) mayor, who was the guest of honour. His foster family were also in the audience, two lovely people who I had got to know really well, and proof that there are unselfish people in our society, prepared to give up their normal life for someone who desperately needs love, understanding, and a stable home base from which to progress.

Foreign students can sometimes bring unexpected bonuses of another sort. Some years ago I found myself having to cover a difficult group of students who, unfortunately for me, had a lesson at a time in the week when through a quirk in the timetable, I had almost half a day of 'prep time'. I was, therefore identified as a prime target by the cover supervisor (I loved her really). The sick teacher was also a good friend of mine and I had regularly assisted with disciplinary and other matters with regard to this class, so I found myself faced with a series of Spanish lessons while the regular teacher recovered from an operation. I do speak one other language, but not Spanish; most of my limited Spanish grammar has been acquired through holidays, 'Dos cervezas gracias' being a prime example, also some words from a Spanish teacher friend who loved being rude to me in front of the students, 'Buenos dias, Abuelo'(good morning, Grandad) and 'Barcelona dos, Chelsea Uno' being typically cheap shots; and the occasional word remembered from the classic song 'Guantanamera' which I have been known to sing after a few too many cervezas!

As an aside, my best-ever attempt at this song was rudely interrupted by a waiter who threw me out of a Spanish restaurant in Kent as I was attempting to serenade the ladies at our P.E. department annual Christmas meal. It seems I shouldn't have taken his guitar off the wall or spilt some food over his sombrero! The warning signs were apparent when we entered an only half-full restaurant, but were immediately ushered downstairs out of sight of the other (sober) customers! Anyway, I digress.

Luckily for me, one of the pupils in the Spanish class had only arrived from Madrid a few months earlier and also spoke fluent English. She was quite a bright girl and soon realised that my first few lessons were a bit of a disaster, with regard to both content and my own lack of ability. Why she was in the class puzzled me slightly, but perhaps she was a dead cert for an A grade in Spanish later on! Anyway, Rosa came to my rescue in a number of ways. Firstly she was confident enough to lead the Spanish reading sections for me while I concentrated on 'police' duties. Secondly she would confirm if an individual had provided a correct answer and finally she became so keen on her new status as teacher 'numero uno' that she started to provide some excellent visual materials, films and photos about Spain, which definitely perked up the class and their interest in the subject.

One of my most difficult lessons of the week had become quite enjoyable and even my Spanish had improved to such an extent that I was able to counter the aforementioned Spanish teacher's digs with a few choice words of my own, which I often punctuated with some flamenco steps in front of his class and a parting 'Ole!' as I left with matadorial majesty.

There was, however, a sting in this tale! The head of department had become so impressed with the fact that this class were actually doing some work with me that she came to watch one day. I naturally let the whole staffroom know that my teaching skills had risen to new levels with my rapid grasp and sure delivery of this subject and so the verdict on this lesson was eagerly awaited.

Rosa had been suitably primed to bring in a great film about the tourist industry in Spain and we had prepared the lesson perfectly, except for one important detail that will soon become evident. Anyway, the introduction went very well and the quick-fire question and answer session made the H.O.D. sit up in her chair with the accuracy of the replies. The timing of the film was also just right as the group's concentration was beginning to wane. I noticed with relief that quiet and focus had returned as a family group splashed and swam on the screen. A child building sandcastles brought some 'Oh, isn't he sweet' remarks from the girls and then as I looked around, the boys had suddenly become very animated with some eyes even popping out, accompanied by some unsuitable comments about the fairer sex. I swivelled to see to my horror a row of topless beauties marching seductively towards the camera, their bodily details becoming ever more apparent as the camera zoomed in to capture the essentials! I feared the worst as I looked over to the head of department who was shuffling uncomfortably in her seat. The boys' comments were becoming ever more raucous when fortunately the film moved on to a visit to the bullfight.

I was saved! Or was I? ...As the event unfolded the cameraman seemed intent on showing every gory detail and it was in colour. A few murmurs gradually built up into a steady 'boo' against the matador and cheers as one of the picadors was hurled into the air (he lived). The disruption to the lesson was complete when two animal-loving students burst out into tears and one told me they were going to 'tell their mum how cruel I was'. I subsequently received two letters of complaint and a justified grilling from not only the head of languages, but also two senior teachers. Far worse were a torrent of sarcastic comments and other cheap shots I received from the staffroom 'Mafia'. To this day I still don't know who put a copy of page three of *The Sun* in my pigeon hole with the accompanying message, 'You might find this material useful for your Spanish lessons'. The morals: 1. Never show a film or picture without checking the content first. 2. Don't brag about a potentially good lesson in advance!

Before leaving this section I must say a few words about the many teachers from abroad I have worked with over the years. These include the regular supply of Australians, South Africans and Canadians from 'the Colonies', but also in recent years a considerable influx from the EU and many other parts of the world.

They often bring a refreshing air to the daily routine and also a different perspective to our education system. I found that nearly all of them enjoy a bit of friendly banter about the differences between our cultures and they find our stereotyping of their national characteristics hilarious!

As I think about the last few words of this chapter while invigilating an exam, I am in an assembly hall with its fair share of students from abroad. They help to make the school a colourful, lively mix of individuals and cultures; and in the corner out of sight of the students is an Australian teacher demanding my attention by mimicking the catch which won an Ashes test match for Australia the day before!

The Good Lesson

The lesson had finished and as it was breaktime the boys and girls were leaving considerably faster than if they had to go to another class. I had thoughts of doughnuts and coffee, so I proceeded to quickly pack away a few text books and return some pencils to the nearest shelf. Out of the corner of my eye I noticed James lingering at the door, joking with a few friends as they left and glancing at me once or twice in a suspicious way. Eventually, after everyone had left, James had a quick look up and down the corridor and then came back in to the classroom.

I had a sense of foreboding as he approached me. There were only so many doughnuts and the staff queue sometimes got so long that there was hardly any time to enjoy break if you were at the back! Also, James didn't like history and was a very bright, but disruptive pupil, who we used to call 'Rumpole' as he inevitably argued quite eloquently and at great length about any situation that involved him doing anything, with homework being the biggest 'moan'. It was amazing how many visiting aunts and uncles made it impossible for him to study some evenings, and his room must have been decorated three or four times a year! I quickly made myself look busy and in a hurry, but he continued to approach as in my mind a doughnut seemed to be melting away.

To my surprise he said, 'Sir, I really enjoyed that lesson. It was different and it was very interesting to hear about your grandad's experiences in the First World War.' Slightly stunned at this unexpected praise, I thanked him and then asked him what else was good about the lesson (his words had even made me forget my stomach). 'Well, I liked it when you played the recording of the sounds of the trenches as we listened to your grandad's diary and the bit of film at the end was much better than just reading about it.' I thanked him once more for his comments and after a few more words he started to leave again. I sat back luxuriating in the moment rather than bothering about food and drink, when suddenly he turned again and said, 'Could I borrow your grandad's diary for a few days? I'd like to read it all and my dad would like to see it as well; he's really into war stories.' I was only too pleased to lend it to him and added that there was no hurry to return it. He checked the door again quickly before thanking me and saying, 'Sir, would you mind not telling the rest of the class that I borrowed the diary, I don't want them to think I am turning into a boffin!' The rest of my day went really well and I even made an extra effort with a difficult class I had on the 'graveyard shift'.

So what makes a good lesson? A talented and knowledgeable teacher? Great research and preparation? A passion for the subject that captures the audience? Or should we measure lesson quality by exam results at the end of the year? Two constants must be enjoyment and learning, but further than this the good lesson is an elusive beast.

At one end of the spectrum is the following story about an English teacher who I thought looked unusually cheerful, considering he had just had his Monday morning nightmare class, a low ability set who not only largely refused to work, but also hated the current topic, a Shakespeare play. I must admit to sometimes joining in the light-hearted ribbing of this teacher in and around the staffroom on occasions about the imminent arrival of this awful group. Only that morning I had joined him as he looked out of the staffroom window at a wet and cold January morning, no doubt wishing he was still tucked up in bed and not teaching the class from hell in five minutes. I put a hand round his shoulder and pronounced 'Now is the winter of our discontent!' I couldn't repeat his next few words here, but his mood was not improved when the bell sounded and as he was about to leave the staffroom, another 'villain' shouted out, 'Once more into the breach!' So why was he looking so cheerful only a few minutes after the lesson? Our usual post 'battle' conversations involved maybe an apology about my latest bad Shakespeare joke and then from him a list of the incidents and punishments resulting from the lesson, coupled with despair and confusion about what to do next. But here he was, quietly whistling away with a contented air. Thinking he had finally been pushed over the edge by Sharon, Jake and the rest I approached cautiously, apologised for my latest Shakespearian wind-up and asked him if he was OK. 'Never better, thanks,' was the surprising reply. Puzzled, I asked him about the English lesson. 'Oh, it went great today. I bribed them with sweets and promised that they could watch a video on the last day of term if no one had a fight and they all stayed in the classroom; it worked a treat!' Unfortunately, the novelty of these rewards wore off after only about three weeks and the teacher concerned had to resort to following more traditional and acceptable ways of trying to control the little love-lies. A 'good lesson' with this class was as basic as no one being lost or killed!

A history teacher from my second school was known as a real risk-taker in the classroom. When confronted with a bored class facing 'Religious Martyrs of the Middle Ages' he decided to kindle some interest. I happened to be walking past his classroom as I noticed some smoke seeping under the door into the corridor. I resisted the temptation to jump up and down shouting 'Fire!'à la Basil Fawlty and instead peered through the window to appraise the situation. In the centre of the room was a dustbin full of old paper and bits of wood, blazing away to such a degree that the boys and girls who were surrounding it were inching away from the intense heat. Grabbing a fire extinguisher I rushed into the room, aimed it at the blaze and was about to soak myself (Basil again, it was pointed in the wrong direc-tion) when the teacher shouted out, 'Stop Mr Foster, it's part of the lesson!' Seeing that the contents did not look like spilling out at that moment I asked him what he meant. 'We're studying martyrs and someone asked about what it must have felt like to be Joan of Arc ... So I thought I'd show them!' By now the fire was dying down and still contained in the dustbin. The class, realising the school was not going to burn down were now booing so loudly that the headmaster (whose office was quite close by) arrived to put a final 'damper' on proceedings by using the extinguisher instantly and correctly. The teacher mysteriously disappeared at the end of term. 'Pity, his lessons were not the usual boring stuff,' remarked one of the class members on hearing he had left.

Shock, or unconventional tactics can work, however, as I found out one day with another history class. I was having a considerable amount of trouble with a pupil who was so disruptive that it was becoming difficult to teach effectively. He was one of the biggest boys in the year and a good sportsman, but not particularly bright and covered his lack of ability by behaving outrageously at every opportunity. Today's lesson was no exception as he bombarded me with silly questions, made rude noises when my back was turned as I was writing on the board and denying that the paper planes that were flying round the room were anything to do with him. His most effective weapon, however, was to slip into rapid 'street talk' or rapping, which I not only didn't understand, but the class (who were otherwise very well behaved) found hilarious. I subsequently found out from a staff meeting that he was doing everything he could to be expelled and that even the most senior teachers in the school found him uncontrollable, but this reassurance that it wasn't just me who was having difficulty was not going to help me for the next few lessons while his future was being sorted out and I was beginning to 'lose' the class. Even his removal to the 'sin bin' was often accompanied by a performance designed to render further effective teaching very difficult.

At the end of the lesson one of the nicest girls asked me if I would give her some advice about the homework. She had, however, other reasons for staying. 'Sir,

Jason's spoiling all our lessons, we're not learning any-thing and he's an idiot. You do your best but he ain't listening. Why don't you make him look small with some aggressive street talk of your own!' I would nor-mally not shout at a pupil and disliked confronting them on a personal level, but decided to give this idea a try. I was also given some real help with suitable phrases by the girl and proceeded to rehearse my body language and hand movements in front of the mirror after the morning shave for a couple of days before the next history lesson.

And so judgement day arrived. As the class settled down I received a reassuring wink from my 'coach' and proceeded with the lesson. It was only a few minutes before a small boy suddenly found his pen had gone missing. I approached the situation in a fairly low-key manner to start off with, but it did not reappear. A few minutes later the boy began to cry as his pen had been returned (while I was writing on the board), broken in half. He was so outraged that he immediately told me it was Jason, who leapt into a tirade about how I always believe everyone in the class except him, plus he was 'going to get the little rat later'. I reassured him that I had not accused him of anything yet, but asked him to comment on the other boy's accusation. 'You're always picking on me, Foster!' was quickly followed by a chair being knocked over and a rush of super-fast street talk that was even more rapid than usual.

My response was instant. I jumped out of my seat, pulled out a baseball cap, swung it round to the rear and leant to the side, imitating a move I had studied on an Eminem video I saw the previous evening. I then strode quickly over to him complete with exaggerated swagger and pronounced, 'You's vexing me Jason! Bro, I don't like you dissing my lesson!' I then clicked my fingers, folded my arms with a suitable flourish and stared him out. For a few moments silence reigned, then the whole class started to laugh out loud. Success or disaster? Jason looked round, took in the situation and then stood up, mumbled a few words, went to the back of the class and slumped head in hands for the rest of the lesson. We never spoke again apart from the register call, but in the two further months he lasted at the school, he just sat quietly and reluctantly did a little bit of work. It seems that the shock of my actions and the class laughing had made him lose street cred with his 'tough' mates and he didn't want to risk further humiliation.

In the weeks after the lesson a number of the class came up to me and congratulated me on the 'result' with Jason's behaviour. I even received a few highfive and 'Yo, Fos' combinations.

Whilst on the subject of rapping and rhyming, I sometimes used these as 'fun' finishes to a lesson, or a time-filler if the lesson had finished too early. I can also thoroughly recommend them as an occasional home-work task. In the classroom, the performance can be made even better if you can get hold of a 'beat box' recording, some girl soloists for the choruses and a deep-voiced boy for the base sections. Below are two of my favourite history 'raps' and a poem. One of them is from me and the others are from two year nine pupils. I won't tell you which one is mine (because it's the best).

The Battle of Hastings Rap
I'm gonna tell you' bout sixty-six
Old Eng-e-land was in a fix
There was Harold The Brit and Will-i-am
Both trying to prove they could be the man

Chorus
Girls: Hastings! Hastings!
Bass: Boo boo boo boo
Boo boo boo boo boom
Girls: Hastings! Hastings!
Bass: Yo, check it out!

Now the axes and swords were beginning to rattle
Everyone was ready for a massive battle
Harold the Brit was on a hill
His soldiers itching for the kill

But Will-i-am had worked things fine
He knew just how to break the line
His horsemen turned and ran away
The Brits thought they had won the day

Chorus
So down the hill rushed Harold's men
But the Normans turned and charged again
The fight was close but the Saxons lost
Old Eng-e-land would count the cost

Now Harold didn't run away
His best men also wanted to stay
They fought with pride with swords on high
Till an arrow struck Harold in the eye

Hastings! Hastings!
Boo boo boo boo
Boo boo boo boo boom
Hastings! Hastings!
Yo, check it out! ... In The Bayeux Tapestry

The next example is not a rap but a poem based on Wordsworth's 'Daffodils'. It was produced during an English cover lesson where the class had been so good, I thought they deserved a bit of fun at the end after nearly an hour of mostly copying about famous British poets.

Wordsworth in London
I wandered lonely in the crowd
That walked up Bromley Hill
When all at once I heard some shouts
from my mates Jim and Phil
They turned their heads and looked so pleased
With hair all flowing in the breeze.

We looked up at the stars that shine
And said what we had done that day
Then suddenly we saw a line
Of people in a happy way
A hundred saw I at a glance
They must be queuing for a dance!

I said to Phil let's go that way
I'm sure they'll take another three!
Jim said 'But I'm too old and grey
To be in such young company'
He fussed and fussed but little thought
About the friends that he had brought

Then suddenly – I tell no lie!
He saw me in a pensive mood
I looked up to his twinkling eye
And knew that he would be a dude
So soon our hearts with pleasure filled
As we danced with Shirley, Debs and Jill.

<u>The Suffragettes Story</u>
This is my story so please take note
It's about those girls that had no vote
There was Anne, Jane and Emeline
Together they really made a scene
The Gov-ern-ment began to fret
About those troublesome Suffragettes

Chorus
Suffering suffering Suffragettes
Suffering suffering Suffragettes
Suffering suffering Suffragettes
They suffered – to get the vote

They re-alised that words were failing
So tied themselves up to some railings
With bars and stones they smashed doors down
And marched all through old London Town
The police they started to get rough
They'd show the girls that they were tough

Chorus
To prison they were dragged and pulled
Some papers wrote that they were fools
But the girls they hadn't finished yet
They were well hard those Suffragettes.
Some started up a hunger strike
And others marched on a long hike

Chorus
Do you wonder how my story ends?
Well the girls they started to make friends
In World War One they worked real hard
In factories and in the yard
The leaders started to take note
And gave the girls the winning vote

Suffering suffering Suffragettes
Suffering suffering Suffragettes
Suffering suffering Suffragettes
They suffered – but got the vote

But winning a battle against a difficult pupil, or adding some unusual or fun elements does not mean that the whole lesson has been great. So let me continue my search for a really good lesson.

Is preparation the key? I have huge admiration for a teacher, particularly in academic subjects, who manages to keep up with all their marking (sometimes up to ten sets of thirty books each), complete all the weekly admin, deal with any pastoral problems that occur in their form group and still prepare top-notch lessons. They must survive on practically no sleep!

Some years ago I was asked to observe and report on a series of science lessons taken by three probationary teachers. They were required to provide me with a detailed lesson plan at least three days before the lesson containing aims and objectives, accurate timings for each section of the lesson, differentiated work for students of higher or lower ability ... and much more...ouch!

As I read through the first of these lessons I became more and more impressed with its good learning objectives, excellent content, precise timings and changes of pace and type of activity. This was going to be a good one! I read through the names in the class and also realised that this was not only a top set but a class containing some of my favourite students. My cup of cocoa was finished with a satisfied sigh and I tucked myself in for a good night's sleep.

The lesson was at 11a.m. two days later. This was also a good time as by then most of the pupils had usually got over any early morning sleepiness, but were not yet fed up with, or exhausted from a whole day at school. I made sure I was a few minutes early and answered a few inevitable 'What are you here for?' questions. The class were lined up silently and as the teacher arrived he had merely to nod and they entered silently and moved to a clearly designated seat (I made good comments in the 'discipline' and 'organisation' sections of my report sheet). The register was also completed impeccably.

The introduction involved a recap of the knowledge gained from the previous lesson (electric currents) and to his credit the teacher did not chose one of the class superstars to summarise this verbally; so I was again impressed when 'Mr average pupil' gave a very good account of what had happened.

It was then that things started to drift downhill.

I was slightly surprised when a second, third and fourth pupil were also asked to summarise the last lesson. I thought that this might be because number one had missed something out, but five minutes later we had just had the same information four times! I glanced over to one of the boys in the class who returned my gaze with eyes knowingly raised and a stifled yawn. I began to worry, but put down the past few minutes to the teacher making sure some key points were well and truly 'rammed home'. I took a little stroll round and noticed that these points had been copied into the exercise book and highlighted during the last lesson. So I was surprised when the overhead projector shone out with exactly the same words and the teacher instructed everyone to copy it down again (unnecessary repetition was entered onto my sheet).

The lesson then moved on to its main theme, which involved the construction of a circuit complete with batteries, wires and switches etc. I felt sure that this activity would liven up proceedings, but was horrified to see that it was only the teacher who was going to demonstrate the experiment and that ten at a time were going to watch. The rest were asked to copy some more information from the OP while they waited, very bored. Now, if it had been an experiment involving dangerous chemicals, or an explosion, I could have seen the need for caution (not to mention health and safety), but this was not dangerous and the boys and girls were not the sort who would want to nick a battery!

I took in some more knowing glances from the students and pretended to be making some notes to disguise my boredom and dissatisfaction and fifteen or so minutes later the class sat down to write up the results of an experiment that had been done for them and contained little mystery or discovery.

I looked at the lesson notes and realised that the words on the sheet with regard to timing etc. indeed related to activities that occurred in the lesson, but the reality for the pupils was something completely different. I almost contributed to the problems by nodding off for a second, but my slide off a stool was halted by a boy who was returning from the experiment observation. I bounced off him and pretended it was a joke nudge. He laughed, moved on and I just about got away with this very unprofessional conduct!

After a few more minutes the lesson ground to a conclusion and I was glad that the teacher had another lesson straight away, which gave me a few hours to create some constructive criticism for our post-lesson meeting.

A few nights later, I nearly choked on my cocoa when I realised that the second and third lessons were with pupils from the same year and that the topic was identical. I made a mental note to have a couple of strong coffees and a bracing shower before the next 'event'. The preparation notes were also worryingly similar. Impressive, yes … but look what happened last time!

Also, the class were not the 'A Team' by any measure and I had had a recent argument with one of the worst behaved boys about some totally inappropriate P.E.

kit. I had even humiliated him a little by commenting that his Bermuda shorts made him look like an extra from *Baywatch*.

I approached the class just after they had entered, to avoid a possible disturbance with David Hasselhoff and sat down with some trepidation.

My spirits were lifted when the recap session was handled completely differently. The teacher had prepared a Power Point presentation with key words missing. The class provided these with a quick-fire hands-up session and then we moved seamlessly into the experiment, which was carried out in smartly selected pairs. The teacher kept a watchful eye on proceedings, but also assisted the slower learners effectively and discreetly. The whole section was also imbued with a sense of fun and discovery and the rest of the lesson also involved a variety of tasks and regular changes of speed. It was so good I had to double check the lesson notes with the unfortunate first lesson and sure enough they were quite similar, but the interest, learning and fun in the second lesson were light years ahead of the first.

The third lesson on the same subject was distinctly lacking in written preparation, but the teacher was a 'natural' who the kids absolutely loved. I got so involved in the lesson that I started to join in by helping one or two groups during the experiment phase and had to force myself back to my notes and observation. There was a lot of fun, laughter and learning in this hour and I found the whole experience quite uplifting. I also learnt a lot from the teacher as with the previous lesson.

I thought that the post-lesson meeting with the teacher would be tricky with regard to the lack of written preparation, but after just a few minutes' discussion it was obvious that this teacher had every-thing ready in her head and just needed to add this detail on paper for future observation sessions. She was also brilliant at thinking on her feet. At one point the lesson momentarily started to flag just slightly. I watched her take the situation in as she scanned the classroom and before a potentially disruptive pupil could shift an inch, she had them back in the palm of her hand with a brilliant and fun adaption of the current section of work. I was enjoying myself so much I also whispered a possible idea into her ear. A minute later she said, 'Mr Foster could you come over here and help me with this pupil?' 'Give us a kiss and I'll think about it' was my reply, which got a good laugh and a nice round of applause from the class before they slipped seamlessly back into work mode.

Good preparation can come in various forms but can rarely be ignored if the lesson is going to be a success. But if the teacher doesn't have the ability to engage the class the lesson will not hit the heights.

Pupils can also spot an insincere teacher at fifty yards. They seem to have a sixth sense which tells them if a teacher isn't really interested in their progress or welfare or doesn't really want to be there. And a teacher trying to be tough when it is not really their style can often be met with ridicule by the class. The best disciplinarians I have ever come across don't even have to speak when they enter a classroom. They have something about them that perhaps can't be learnt. They are also respected because they are firm, fair, consistent and have a sincere attitude to educating and supporting young people.

A good lesson is a combination of a number of factors. The teacher must have a good knowledge of their subject and be able to deliver the content in an interesting way that will also increase the students' learning. The best teachers I have met are charismatic, even though they may have quite different personalities and teaching styles. They have respect from the pupils because the boys and girls know exactly how they are expected to behave and the consequences of poor behaviour and they recognise that the teacher has a genuine interest in them as individuals.

When James told me that he had enjoyed my lesson it was one of those moments that make teaching one of the most rewarding professions in the world. You get a good feeling about yourself and what you are doing in life and also a sense that you are helping the next generation to develop an interest in a subject you love. Who knows, I might even have taught a good lesson!

The School Pantomime

It's the chapter about the school panto.
Oh no it isn't!
Oh yes it is!
It started in 1998.
It's behind you!
And I often played a villain.
Hiss, boo!

Sorry, I'll start this chapter again...It's just that I still get very excited about this event which was watched by the lower school on the last day of the Christmas term, with about twenty of the teachers acting and the staff 'supergroup' providing the music in the intervals. The first panto (*Cinderella*) came about for a number of reasons.

From about 1985 till 1996 I had organised a staff review, which began after the students had gone home early on the last day of term. Following the inevitable goodbyes to a few members of staff who were leaving at Christmas, we would all relax with some food and a few drinks to be followed by the 'entertainment', which could be a song or a dance, but more usually a sketch by a few individuals or members of a department, often taking the mickey out of another section of the staff, but always in the best possible taste!

Some examples of the P.E. department's best efforts were 'Los Physicalos', a flamenco group that contained some talented dancers, but also, deliberately, an awful singer (me) and a terrible guitar player. I can't sing and my accompaniment consisted of the few Spanish words I knew repeated over and over again and meaning absolutely nothing! The guitarist, meanwhile, strummed away merrily but had no idea how to play the instrument. The audience seemed stunned at first (a bit like *The Producers*) but then seemed to realise that we were not to be taken seriously and it went down quite well.

Another offering a few years later was a direct response to a big push on careers advice that year which we called 'When I grow up'. This consisted of a succession of performers singing a description of a typical day in their chosen professions, which included a female dancer whose act seemed to involve clothes coming off, a surgeon whose carefully-enacted operation turns into a bloodbath, and yours truly as a fireman, swinging his hose around (in the best possible taste).

In the mid-1990s we even introduced a judging panel complete with gorgeous lady (Fifi l'Amour, the French teacher) and the resident Simon Cowell who was really nasty to some of the acts.

This format really livened up the end of term and we would often still be laughing about some of the acts hours later in the pub.

All good things come to an end however, and by the late '90s it was time for a change. I consulted a few members of staff about a karaoke and they seemed to be keen. The headmaster gave his approval and I lined up some talented singers from the staff to get things off to a great start.

The final day of term arrived, the children were dispatched off home, a few drinks had loosened up the crowd and we were ready to go … except that the first two people I had organised to sing shrunk into the background when I requested a volunteer. I made a couple more jovial requests, but to my horror no one moved. It was left to the worst singer on the staff to get things going! Being an Elvis fan I selected 'All Shook Up' and proceeded to pound this out to the best of my ability. There was some uncomfortable mumbling at the end of this disaster so I quickly moved on to 'Blue Christmas', fully expecting everyone to join in with the festive spirit, but at the end of this 'destruction' of a great song the crowd were inching even further away and drifting back into embarrassed conversation. I made one more plea for a real singer before 'naming and shaming' the two who had let me down in one last desperate attempt to spur them into action. This did not have the desired result either, so I decided to give up and, instead switched on some canned music. As I went over to grab a much-needed drink the machine blew up, complete with a puff of smoke. At which point everyone laughed out loud. I was deciding whether to 'do a Basil' or not when I suddenly saw the funny side of the situation myself. As I passed the headmaster he commented, 'What are you planning next year, Peter?'. And thus ended the karaoke experiment!

The final factor in the birth of the panto was the fact that there didn't seem to be any organised 'fun' for the pupils at the end of the Christmas term. A few teachers had parties and if they had been very good, a select band of one hundred per cent attenders, for example, might get to visit a Christmas tree farm. But the reality for the majority of the boys and girls was somewhat different. I knew this at first hand because I was still a head of year in 1997and it fell to the year heads to walk round the school and dismiss the classes when they had their room tidy and were suitably well behaved. This was fine in theory, except that there was always a wide range of activities going on and also a variety of attitudes from their form tutors.

So as I approached my first class at the allotted departure time I opened the door to a party still in progress, complete with music and wild dancing. After receiving a kiss from the lady teacher under the mistletoe, I told her that I would come back in about fifteen minutes to dismiss the class. The second form room presented a very different scene. The very strict form tutor had made his class tidy up etc. a long time before the final bell and they were sitting in complete silence (Christmas spirit?). Anyway, I wished them a merry Christmas, dismissed them and then listened to a few individuals moaning about their form tutor as they left.

The next class were also perfectly quiet, but this did not disguise a mountain of litter under their feet and tables. I reluctantly informed the form tutor that they would have to tidy up before leaving and moved on to the next 'experience' which was relatively pleasant.

I was, however, left with the distinct impression that the majority of pupils were leaving school at Christmas in a disappointed mood, whilst a few had openly complained about the 'miserable' teachers and school.

An idea was beginning to form in my head. I had heard about school pantomimes from teacher friends and how much fun they could be. It would also provide a 'controlled' end to the Christmas term with the pupils hopefully enjoying watching the teachers make fools of themselves and the spectating teachers also having fun and being thankful for an hour in the great hall at the end of term, rather than a stressful time in their classroom. The idea was given the green light by the head and the following October I was swamped with budding 'luvvies' wishing to volunteer for the big event.

The panto was born!

For the next day or two there was a nice atmosphere in school with a number of teachers coming up to me with positive comments about the panto idea and others volunteering to be in the performance etc. There was even a group of musicians who were constantly talking about the formation of the 'supergroup'. On the third day a member of staff came up to me and asked for the script ... and suddenly it dawned on me that this new idea would either require me to find a suitable script, or write one myself! I felt quite confident about selecting a cast and directing the show but would the kids find a straight copy of *Cinderella* funny, or would it be better to adapt the story to include references to the school, teachers and perhaps some current TV shows and celebs? I decided on the latter course and sat down to study the original story and then substitute a whole lot of bad jokes about nasty teachers and good looking ones etc, until about two weeks later scenes one and two were ready. I had already sent out a message to all the staff asking for volunteers and the response had been excellent (well, it was the first one). Even this letter contained some examples of the childish humour that was to characterise this and other productions, e.g. 'Join us for some panto fun ... Yule have a great time!'

I handed out the scenes to a few of the cast at breaktime and waited nervously for some chuckles. It was to my great relief that some were smiling and others even laughing, but my head shrunk a little when one of the potential stars exclaimed 'The kids will love this rubbish!'

There were to be eight rehearsals with the last one being a full dress event. I reminded everyone about rehearsals at practically every staff meeting complete with the latest news about who was going to be Cinderella etc. and even a pantomime tradition began to develop in these staff meetings. For example, I might say 'I would like to remind everyone in the panto that there is a rehearsal on Thursday'. At which point about half the staff would shout out 'Oh no there isn't!' 'And can I remind you that it will end later than last week.' 'Hiss! Boo!'

As an aside, it seems that my panto announcements at the staff meeting also served another purpose. A few years later I was becoming a little puzzled with some conflicting remarks from certain members of staff. Generally speaking I probably made an announcement about the panto at least once a week so I was a little surprised when the head of history came up to me and said 'Pete, I'm not sure you're mentioning the panto enough. They may forget a rehearsal or lose interest. Don't forget to mention it at the next staff meeting!' I was a little confused as I was sure I had mentioned it at both staff meetings that week, so I went over to a member of the cast I thought I could trust and asked his opinion on the frequency of these announcements. The teacher concerned asked me who had made this observation and I told him. Without hesitation he responded, 'He doesn't know what he's talking about. I think quite a few teachers are getting fed up with the panto announcements. In fact I wouldn't say anything at all next week!' This left me even more confused. The pattern continued over the next few weeks with a surprising number of teachers taking an interest in staff meetings and what I was going to say. Eventually, with only one week to go before the performance, the head of history pronounced, 'It's vital that you mention the panto twice this week. Don't forget!'

I subsequently found out that he had set up a betting ring on how many times I would mention the panto at staff meetings between the beginning of November and December 17 (the performance date). His own estimate was considerably more than my average for the first few weeks, so his 'encouragement' to mention the subject more often was based on him potentially winning about £30. I am glad to say that he was not the lucky winner! The teacher I had consulted was also in on the bet, but had chosen a much smaller number for my estimated announcements total. That's why he wanted me to say nothing for a week (he didn't take the money either).

It was the afternoon of the first-ever pantomime rehearsal. I was first into the great hall at the end of the school day, which is a terrific venue, having a good size stage and seating for about 500. In addition, the hall itself resembles a Victorian theatre, with fine columns and ornate plasterwork, plus a plush velvet-like curtain.

I had provided drink and refreshments for the ensemble and had received some encouraging comments from the artistes about how they were looking forward to the first rehearsal. Bang on time three or four arrived, script in hand. We had a few preliminary discussions about this and that while we waited for the rest...About ten minutes passed, then fifteen, without any further arrivals. After twenty minutes I apologised to those present and informed them that I would go and chase up all the rest. And thus started the only regular 'moan' concerning the panto (apart from not learning lines). The cast just didn't turn up on time, apart from a few regular stalwarts, or had just forgotten about it. If it had been a staff meeting they would all have been there, but the panto just didn't have the same clout and the headmaster wasn't going to tell you off for missing a panto rehearsal.

Just when I thought that Cinderella had died before her Prince had found her, the others began to dribble in. I didn't want to kill everyone's interest, but I did have the first of many moans. Fortunately, about an hour and a half later, we had all had so much fun, I could tell we were on to a winner! After a few inhibitions had been lost we all threw ourselves into rehearsals. The terrible jokes only added to the laughter as did the references to teachers nasty and nice and regular derogatory comments about the pupils.

Sometimes people were off school sick and the actors had to take on more than one part in order that the rehearsal could proceed. I remember getting a little agitated once when the Prince wasn't really 'in character' at one rehearsal. He very sharply reminded me that as he was actually only the curtain operator I was lucky that he was doing the part at all (or words to that effect)!

The final dress rehearsal went reasonably smoothly and we all enjoyed listening to the band playing in the intervals. The fact that it was a full dress rehearsal added to the excitement as it was the first time we had seen everyone in their costumes and I was amazed how much trouble (and in some cases expense) everyone had taken to look the part.

The big day arrived. The performers mostly arrived on time, but it was a little worrying that some were still learning their lines. Another nervous artiste came up to me and checked which side they should enter from and Prince Charming asked me if it was all right if he turned on the passion a bit more on the final kiss with Cinders; two of the cast and the curtain operator hadn't even turned up, but apart from that everything was perfect!

I peeped out from behind the curtain to see a full hall of expectant and lively children. I thought however, that the faces on some of the supervising teachers looked a little stern and the headmaster was looking at his watch. I came out from behind the curtains and spoke to the audience for a few minutes about having fun and how to behave etc. and then led a few practice 'Boos' to warm them up for the start. I then announced the staff supergroup who were to play an introductory song before the first act, but no one appeared! A kind teacher rushed out to the playground where one or two were still having their final cigarette before facing the hoardes. Fortunately their entrance was only delayed for a few seconds ... and then we were off! I waited behind the curtains as the storyteller set the scene and the play began. To my relief there was lots of laughter almost from the start and everyone seemed to have remembered their lines. It was halfway through scene one and my big moment! I hadn't had a dress on for years, so from quite early I had decided to be one of The Ugly Sisters. The other Ugly Sister was quite small as I thought this would make quite a nice contrast. Marcus and I waited in the wings for our grand entrance and as 'I'm Too Sexy' blasted out of the speakers, we dangled a leg suggestively around the curtain. We then catwalked towards the audience pausing only to add lipstick and sit on one or two male teacher's knees. There was an initial shock at these two drag queens suddenly appearing, but then (thank goodness) some quite loud laughter!

About an hour and a quarter later the cast were singing Slade's 'Merry Christmas' accompanied by most of the audience and the first Ravensbourne Panto had been a great success. Cinderella was beautiful, Prince Charming had morphed into James Bond, The Fairy Godmother had overacted (the head of drama of course) and hundreds of happy pupils left the hall ... A good time had been had by all! (Oh yes it was!)

On the next page is the first scene of *Cinderella* (Rubbish!) The audience joined in by reading a prompt board.

Scene 1: Cindy at home and unhappy

Directions	Actor	Lines
Curtain closed Story teller in comfy chair to one side(Ronnie Corbett)		
Admonishes teacher in audience	Storyteller	*Hello everyone, when you are sitting comfortably I'll begin our story...This is the sad tale of Cindy, a schoolgirl just a little older than most of you. She was a good girl – which means she didn't go to this school!*
Prompt for audience	Audience Storyteller	*Hiss, Boo!!!!* *But at home she was treated very badly by her mother and sisters...Our story starts with Cindy at home*
Curtain opens. EnterCindy.Storyteller exits. Cindy sweeping floor, chases mice away then sits down amidst piles of homework, looks fed up – opens book.	Cindy	*6 x – 2y + 15d = ? I really don't know! I want to do my maths homework but I'm too tired from all the cleaning! I can't concentrate!*
From off stage right Mum enters (fag, hair curlers etc)	Mum	*Cindy – have you swept the floor, done the ironing and finished your homework? Come on.it's nearly six o clock! I hope you're not slacking again! And where's the dinner?*

Cindy sarcastic	*Cindy*	*Oh sorry Mum. I forgot to show you how to put the chips in the oven!*
	Mum	*Don't you get sarky with me young lady – I didn't bring you into the world to just laze around! Have you seen the TV remote control thingy?*
Cindy holds it up, it was right in front of Mum on the table. She takes it and leaves. *She says on leaving*	*Mum*	*Don't forget, Dinner by seven. I don't want to miss the fashion show on the telly.*
Cindy returns dejected to homework. Enter two ugly sisters stage right to 'I'm Too Sexy'. They prance and strut.	*Gloria*	*Hello, I'm Gloria Thunderthighs and I'm a size 38*
	Audience	*Get off!*
	Shirley	*And I'm Shirley Sex Bomb. I'm size 40 they're inflatable and the boys really love my legs.*
	Audience	*You must be joking!*
She points to selected male teachers in audience laughing, mocking	*Gloria*	*What horrible children! And look, there's some really rough-looking blokes in the audience!*
	Audience	*Applause!*

They pose	Gloria	Hello Cindy – doing your homework? Good girl. Still I think you'll need to do well in your exams. Shirley and me haven't got that problem- we've got the looks!
	Shirley	Yes Cinds, that's why all the good-looking boys will be after us at Saturday's disco- by the way, has anyone invited you?
	Sisters	No...shame!
They leave, laughing Cindy crying Lights dim, close in on Cindy.	Cindy	How can anyone invite me when I don't know anyone – I never go out – I'm always doing all the housework because I'm the youngest and then there's the homework... and it's Christmas and everyone's having fun!
	Audience	Shame!
	Cindy	Oh I've never been so lonely!!
Supergroup play 'Lonely this Christmas'.		

As usual, a number of the teachers went to the pub that evening and it was there that I discovered another 'panto bonus'. About five of the teachers who had taken part were new to the school and it seems that the involvement in rehearsals and the production in general had really helped them to settle in.

The following year was 1999, which gave me a strong urge to choose a panto with a message for the new millennium. For a while I mulled over the possibility of Robin Hood redistributing the wealth from the rich to the poor, but finally settled on *Scrooge 2000* as having a stronger message, plus a clearly-defined happy ending.

This year it was quite easy to recruit people for the show as the novelty factor was still there from the previous year. There was also a group of drama kings and queens developing who used to come and see me with strong hints about the star role they fancied. In particular, Karen was so demanding she actually threatened to pull out of one or two productions unless she was 'the star'! This all added to the staffroom fun and the cast quickly rose to a very healthy thirty-plus.

I had also decided that it would be a good idea if all the music was linked to the story. So after one or two discussions with the supergroup and members of the cast, we settled on a number of songs to do with money and greed. The Beatles provided 'Money, That's What I Want' and 'Hey Scrooge' and I took advantage of the fact that we had a very good sixth-form singer who was also a big ABBA fan, who sang 'It's a Rich Man's World' dressed as one of the ABBA girls. To make sure the message about greed was well and truly rammed home we all sang 'Imagine' at the end, before the final Christmas pop classic rounded off proceedings.

One of my best chums, Malcolm, had only agreed to be in the panto after much arm pulling and cajoling. I had also tried to 'con' him into the show by arranging for a few other teachers to mention how good he would be as Bob Scratchit (the family were so poor they suffered from fleas), but this only made things worse as he worked out that this was a set up. I tried one last idea by suggesting that it would be quite funny if I tailored the role of Scratchit for a northern accent as he was from Yorkshire. He could then publicly blame this departure from a Cockney character on the scriptwriter, moi. The idea of having a go at me in public definitely appealed to him and he was 'in'. Here is that section from the script. Oh, by the way, Tiny Tim was played by a six-foot P.E. teacher.

Directions	Actor	Lines
Storytelling group in front of curtain (right).	*Dad*	*Our story moves to the Scratchit's house, where Sarah and her husband Bob live with their young son Tiny Tim. It's an old, small place because they couldn't afford anything better.*
	Son	*I bet they didn't drive a Skoda like you, Dad!*
Dad slaps son on head. They exit (stage right). Sad music (Hovis theme). Curtain opens Sarah's buttering bread – looks up–Bob enters.		
	Sarah	*Hello Bob, you're a bit late back from work?*
Heavy northern accent – plucks braces.	*Bob*	*Aye, sorry lass … There was trouble in mill!*

He sits down.	*Sarah*	*What do you mean mill? You work in a biscuit factory ... and why are you speaking in a strange northern accent? This is London!*
	Bob	*I don't know pet. It must be script writer getting the story mixed up.*
	Sarah	*Yeh, I think you're right. What do you think of the story so far kids?*
	Audience	*Rubbish*
	Sarah	*Bob, something terrible happened at the office today!*
	Bob	*Aye, it's grim up north! Is there any black pudding lass?*
	Sarah	*Oh, I give up! Anyway Bob, I'm worried about Christmas. There's no money again – Mr Scrooge hasn't increased my wage for five years. The telly's about to break down and I can't even afford a proper Christmas meal for Tiny Tim!*
Bob looks to side stage (left). Tim enters – Sarah kisses him. He wipes mouth.	*Audience*	*Oh, shame!*
	Tim	*Yugh!*

Tim turns on telly– very upset, cries.	*Tim*	*Hello Mummy, Daddy!*
	Tim	*Oh Mummy, Daddy, boo, hoo! No Teletubbies – telly no good, boo hoo!*
Tim sulks to table.	*Sarah*	*Sorry Tim – never mind, come and have your dinner.*
Sarah breaks down, tears, slumps into seat at table.	*Tim*	*Bread – yuk! Soup – yuk! Don't want this! Want Big Mac – double fries!*
	Bob	*This is all that evil Scrooge's fault – why can't he pay you more? It's Christmas and in a few days it's new millennium!*
Tim sobs quietly – Sarah recovers – Tim sucks thumb.	*Sarah*	*No Bob! We mustn't talk like that about Mr Scrooge. I feel sorry for him. He may have lots of money – but no family or friends like us and I'm sure he's never had a girlfriend.*
They exit with Tim sobbing– curtain closes – interval song–'It's a Rich Man's World'	*Bob*	*Aye lass, all right…but I bet he doesn't sleep well at night. All that money he takes from poor folk… It's grim but true pet – aye – it's a rich man's world!*

Scrooge also contained a new idea that was to remain a regular feature in future pantos, the dance sequence. I had been considering incorporating Michael Jackson's 'Thriller' into the graveyard scene where Scrooge sees his own future gravestone. A number of colleagues thought that my plans were far too ambitious, 'Who do you think you are, Steven Spielberg?' was one response from a non-believer, but it worked out fine on the night, with one dancer coming out of a trapdoor behind Scrooge's grave and the rest, dressed like zombies, entering from all around the hall, suitably scaring the audience and even dancing pretty well. In all future productions there was always at least one big dance.

The year 2000 brought *The Wizard of Oz* with Ali G being the narrator, in his own particular style, 'Innit'!; 2001 was *Snow White* including some reluctant dwarfs who had to spend about an hour on their knees and regular adverts for white products, e.g. Bashful (to Snow White); 'Ooh what a lovely white dress you're wearing!'

TV Ad Man (enters stage left): 'That's because Snow White washes her dress in new Extra White! Just look at this! We washed a pair of Mr Sexton's socks in Daz and look at the result! Still full of dirt and what about the smell? Ooh nasty!

We washed this second pair in new Extra White – look at the difference! No dirt, beautifully white and what about the smell? Mmm, it's fresh and clean with new Extra White!'

Maid (to wicked Queen); 'Snow White is pretty although not as pretty as you...but she does have lovely white teeth!'

TVAd Man (enters stage right); 'That's because Snow White brushes her teeth with new Extra Shine. Once a day and they're clean! Twice a day and you'll need to wear these sunglasses when you watch her smile! ...Yes, your teeth will really shine with new Extra Shine!'

The following year's hosts for *Jack and The Beanstalk* were Posh and Becks, with Victoria more concerned with her clothes and make-up than telling the story. The climax was a rather splendid maypole dance, the pole and ribbons taking hours to make, although I did have a great group of helpers.

It was during the dance rehearsals that I lost my cool.

There were two dances that year and as the real dancers were busy practicing their 'Woodland Nymph' performance, it was left to me to 'direct' the rest of the cast in the maypole dance. I studied some ancient films on the subject which seemed to have been made in a chocolate-box English countryside that doesn't seem to exist any more and then gathered everyone together for the first of three dance rehearsals. The first task was to ask for a volunteer to hold the pole steady for health and safety reasons. There was quite a rush for this job, which made me wonder if anyone really wanted to do the dance! After choosing the least fit member as 'pole person' I moved over to start the music, at which point the whole group started to dance around the pole in chaotic fashion, risking serious damage to the painstakingly constructed ribbons and other adornments. I shouted for them to wait until I showed them 'how to do it' but they continued to merrily tangle each other up in the beautiful construction.

It was a Basil Fawlty moment!

After a couple of uncharacteristic shouts I lined everyone up and proceeded to tell them off, adding that we only had thirty minutes to rehearse the dance and couldn't afford to waste any time.

I think they all realised that I was 'having a moment' so they reluctantly sat back to watch my demonstration of the basic steps to music. In order to preserve the pristine gym floor I removed my shoes and took up the starting position and pronounced 'This is how you do it.' The music started; I grabbed a blue ribbon (blue for boys) and began to dance. After only five steps my socks slipped on the polished floor and I ended up in a heap complete with detached ribbon strung around my neck! There was a moment's silence before Steve came over to check if I was hurt. When it was clear I was not injured he said, 'Is it OK if we laugh then?' at which point twelve teachers could restrain themselves no longer!

I became even more angry for a second or two before relaxing and joining in the laughter. The ensemble, to their credit, subsequently rehearsed the dance very well but I could have done without one or two asking me to show them 'how to do' certain moves in the staffroom for the rest of that week! There was one remaining problem in that the dancers couldn't remember the names for the various step changes they were supposed to do, so I decided to simplify things by given them common, yet descriptive terms. Thus the first three clockwise rotations became known as the 'horsy, horsy' movement and the next anti-clockwise sequence the 'Larry Grayson' as it required a limp wrist held out sideways.

With all these changes of step and direction I wasn't sure if it would go 'all right on the night' so I decided to stand at the back of the stage shouting out 'horsy, horsy' etc, but no one collided with anyone else, they all moved in the correct way and we had a perfectly woven pattern of ribbons around the maypole as the crowd applauded the end of the show!

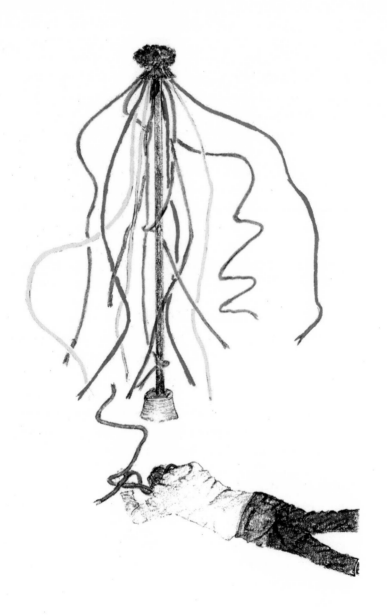

The only other 'dance crisis' in the history of the panto was during *Robin Hood* in 2004 when yours truly was hit around the head with a rather solid stick during the village Morris dancing scene. It was only a small cut and despite mild concussion I managed to finish the scene in one piece.

The following year I decided it was time for a change from the traditional stories and so we decided on a version of *Star Wars*, with Princess Leia being captured and landing on Earth, in fact the school field. This led to some nice banter between some arrogant aliens and a group of girls from the school who just happen to be having a fag behind the sheds.

General (to Kath, as in Catharine Tate); 'If you refuse to kneel in front of Lord Vader, you will be destroyed.'

Kath (to General); 'Do I look as if I'm bovered, metal head?'

In 2006 we returned to more standard fare with *Aladdin*, which also allowed me to get back into a dress again as Widow Twanky.

Widow (to audience); 'As I was saying! I'm Madonna Twankey and I run the Chinese laundry with my two sons Aladdin and Wishee Washee. Actually it's half laundry and half Chinese takeaway ... sort of knickers and noodles...wash while you nosh.'

I also introduced the panto noticeboard that year in the hope that it might provide some fun, but also as another attempt to remind the ensemble of the rehearsal dates as they entered the staffroom (it didn't work). The 'Pantomime Star of the Week' section did, however, raise a few laughs and Jill (in her mid twenties at the time), has kindly allowed me to include her 'moment' in the limelight.

This week's featured Pantomime Star is ... Jill Lengthorne

Exciting! Talented! Good Looking! A bundle of energy!But that's enough about the director, let's look at Jill's pantomime background...

A fresh face not so many years ago, Jill is now an established player on the pantomime scene and still looks far younger than her forty-five years. Always seeking a new challenge, Jill shuns typecasting and has even attempted to play an attractive lady in recent years.

Last year, Jill was a superb Princess Leia in *Star Wars*, bringing great passion to her two lines and five screams. In 2004 she was a soldier in *Robin Hood* and in 2003 flew into theatrical history as Tinkerbell in *Peter Pan*. Her wand-waving only resulted in one serious accident, although we all agreed that Alex Lange looked really cool with a bruised eye for a month!

Jill's role will be very different this year ... hush hush... say no more!

King Arfur and the Knights of the Square Table followed with one of the best dance sequences yet, thanks to two rather flash young male teachers who joined the girls in a tribute to John Travolta.

Sir Drink a lot faints and Arfur asks 'What's wrong with him?'

Merlin; 'Nothing serious, Chief ... I mean Sire. It's been a long week. He's just got a touch of Saturday Knight Fever!' (cue dance group).

In December 2008 I was invited to watch the school panto just a few months after I had retired from full-time teaching. Karen had kindly agreed to take over the organisation of the show (so that she could be star and director!) and I had given her the copies of all the pantos we had done before. It was nice to be in the audience for a change and I had a great afternoon watching Scrooge along with a group of students who were too young to have seen it first time round.

If there are any teachers out there wishing to liven up the end of the Christmas term I can thoroughly recommend the staff putting on a pantomime for as many of the pupils as possible. Yes, the timekeeping of the staff might drive you mad and you will have to devote a lot of energy to encouraging people to take part and building up a script that pokes fun at pupils and teachers, but the reward is to see a lot of happy faces (staff and pupils) leaving school for the start of the festive season! I leave you with Alex's excellent poster for *King Arfur*.

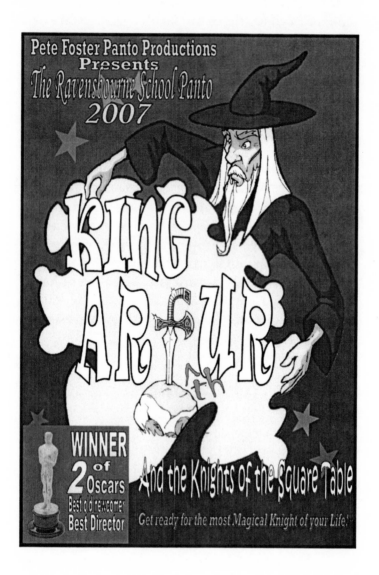

74

Funny Moments

At the bus stop

It had been a good day, my lessons well prepared and with some of the best classes. So it was with a smug, contented, air that I made my way up to the bus stop to catch the 4p.m. bus home. I always looked forward to this trip (especially tonight as I was 'free' considerably earlier than usual having finished all my marking and prep for the next few days well in advance, a rarity) as it took me from the suburban fringes of London out into the rolling North Downs.

The school meal I had eaten a few hours earlier was a delicious salad, reflecting one of my periodic phases of 'healthy eating', but it had left me a little peckish. So much so that my resolve was weakening as I approached the sweet shop en route to the bus stop. I almost made it past, but the shopkeeper ruined my good intentions with a friendly wave and smile. I hesitated for a moment before deciding that it was my duty to support local businesses and went into the shop determined to buy a small but healthy oatmeal bar or suchlike, but I found myself in a queue of two behind a year seven pupil who was buying some jelly babies from a large jar and this brought such fond memories of teeth-rotting joy from my own schooldays that I exited with my own pocketful. (I have since found out that it is possible to buy sugar and fat free jelly babies, which would have made me feel a little less guilty, but such thoughts were nowhere near me as I rewarded myself for a good day's work.)

The first green one tasted so good that I quickly searched for another of the same colour, before moving on to red and other delights.

I noticed with satisfaction that the bus stop was fairly quiet with just one year eight girl who I knew quite well and who I had given a 'credit' to earlier in the day. We exchanged pleasantries and as she was listening to some music with ear plugs in, I relaxed into the next big decision in my life, namely which colour should be next. A minute or so later there was a tap on my shoulder from the girl and this conversation followed...

Girl: 'Sir, are they jelly babies you're eating?'

PF: 'Yup.'

Girl: 'Haven't they got a lot of sugar which isn't good for you?'

PF: (laughing)'No not these ones, they're sugar free.' (A fib.)

Girl: 'Oh, do they taste nice?'

PF: 'Yes, I think so, and there are lots of different flavours.'

Girl: 'Right. 'Cos I wouldn't know, because I've never tried one.'

PF: (Suspecting an attempted raid on the jelly babies;) 'Well good for you. I bet you stick to a really healthy diet. Well done!'

Girl: 'No, I mean I don't know what they taste like because I have never been given one.'(Cue cute smile.)

PF: (Accepting defeat) 'Oh all right then, here, try one.'
Girl: (Straight faced) 'No thanks. My mum told me never to take sweets from strange men!'

The football lesson

My second lesson of the day was year eight football and I wasn't looking forward to it one bit! It wasn't anything to do with the subject, but more a reflection on the weather conditions, which included a temperature close to freezing and a biting wind with the occasional squally shower. I forgot to mention that it was Monday morning and January.

As I walked to the P.E. block I toyed with the idea of suggesting to the head of department that the conditions were so bad it would be more humane to take the class inside, but as I turned the last corner before the changing rooms he was just bringing in a football class himself, so I couldn't be seen to be 'wimping out' in his company. I noticed he didn't even have a tracksuit top or bottoms on as he hurried the group in to get changed and I felt my heart sink as I moved into the staffroom.

As I put my boots on I tried to introduce some positive ideas into my head as a means of distraction from the reality of the next hour. There was the log fire I had prepared the night before at home and then not needed to light as the central heating had done the job; and the last chapter of the excellent book I had been reading awaited me. This vision of curling up in my favourite chair with feet 'toasting' was rudely interrupted by a series of shouts from the boys' changing room. I was by the door in a few seconds and flung it open to be greeted by silence and some surprised looks.

I had learnt that this was often due to some sort of cover-up and proceeded to search up and down a few rows to see if anything, or anybody had been damaged …All clear!

As I was in the room and the lads seemed to be changed I told them to go out and begin jogging slowly round the pitch I had worked out as being slightly sheltered by the main hall of the school and was surprised (considering the conditions) to see them trot out quietly and without any hint of complaint although, again, I received one or two strange stares.

It was freezing and the wind seemed to be picking up, but I had no option but to try and put a brave face on it. As I joined in the warm up, I noticed the head of P.E. gesturing and shouting towards one of the boys. I told him to run over to him and they began a short animated conversation. The boy turned to me, shrugged and then ran back towards me. Salvation! The head was not so tough after all and was calling the group back in due to severe weather conditions. I blew a secret kiss to all the health and safety folk around the globe, but was surprised as he continued past me and continued his warm up. I called to him and asked him what had happened and he just said that he had been told that he had forgotten his packed lunch and his mum was going to leave it at reception.

With all hope gone I gathered the class together and organised them into about five groups for a dribbling and running practice that I hoped would at least stop them from freezing. I had forgotten to consult my notes before the lesson and couldn't be sure what we had done the previous week, but I had been so preoccupied with trying to avoid the elements that this had overridden any thought of a detailed plan for the hour. Anyway, the session went quite well and I then gathered them together to describe one final practice before moving on to a game for the last twenty minutes or so. The group still seemed a little quiet and lacking in enthusiasm, as was I, but at least by the end of the lesson the lads had all had some good exercise and had practised some appropriate skills for the conditions. After taking them back into the changing room and seeing them safely off to their next lesson I settled into to my seat in the P.E. staff room and proceeded to check through some future lesson plans. The only other person in the room was the head of P.E. who was also doing some paperwork. After about five minutes he commented, 'Cold outside, isn't it Pete?' I replied that I didn't think it was so bad (another fib) before adding a few details about the lesson to impress him with my ability to adapt a lesson plan (non existent) to the weather conditions. He asked me how the class had behaved which prompted me to comment on their behaviour being excellent, although they seemed a little quiet, probably due to a reluctance to go out in the cold. He replied, 'Actually, they were probably a bit surprised to see you out there, because you just took my lesson for me! It was your free period. Anyway, thanks a lot, I got a lot of marking done ... Oh, could you leave me the lesson plan so that I know what you covered for the next session!'

Absent minded ... me?

I pride myself on using public transport whenever possible, so I nearly always took a bus to and from school. This also allowed my better half to use the car to get to her work, a much longer and more complicated journey which would otherwise have involved multiple bus changes followed by a long trek down a narrow country lane. I did begrudge the need to get up a little earlier than if I had the car and not being in possession of an MP3 or XYZ or whatever, meant that I couldn't listen to my favourite songs on the bus. Still, on the plus side the smoking ban had made the environment much more pleasant and it was really only rain or cold which made me grumpy.

There was also the possibility that one of the teachers who lived in my village, or passed by it on their route home would be kind enough to give me a lift. If this was arranged earlier in the school day it was even more welcome, especially if the weather was inclement. I must admit to trying to 'cadge' lifts on a regular basis with a winning smile, compliment, or even a bribe such as a doughnut or other treat at breaktime for the unsuspecting driver. Sometimes a lift was even offered which was a bit of a surprise really as the driver inevitably had to listen to a series of terrible jokes, or even worse, yet another instalment of my life story.

One rather wet and windy end of school afternoon, Jackie from the P.E. department asked me if I wanted a lift home.(Perhaps she took pity on me as I looked forlornly out of the staffroom window.)

Jackie was (sorry, is) an extremely accomplished driver, so after a dash across the playground in the rain, it was with a relaxed state of mind that we set off for home. There was even time for one of my 'jokes' at the school gates. We needed to pause to allow some traffic to pass and as Jackie wound a window down to see better, a year nine girl poked her head in and asked me,

'Sir, why are you in a car with Miss Bundy?' to which I replied, 'Well, when you get to my age (fifty-eight) you can't be too choosy!'

There followed a few minutes hold-up while Jackie pretended to order me out of the car (a performance which convinced me that she had sufficient acting potential to be offered a part in the forthcoming school pantomime), but eventually I was forgiven and we were on the way home. I made some quick calculations and worked out that as Jackie had only recently heard chapters five and six of my life story, I would resolve to be unusually quiet on this journey!

After about three miles of the six-mile journey Jackie asked me why I didn't use my car more to come to school. I reminded her about the relative ease of my journey, when suddenly a thunderbolt struck! My wife had not gone to work today as it was an unscheduled day off for her and I had gone to work in the car, which was now sitting in the school car park with no one to bring it home. Worse still, I remembered that I needed to drive my wife to a social 'do' an hour from now so that she could have a few drinks. In a mild state of panic I explained this to Jackie, who following a good laugh and some derogatory comments about my age and fading memory, kindly offered to take me back to school to retrieve my car. This was tempting, but unfair on her, so instead, after a few quick time calculations I asked her to drop me off at the nearest bus stop and thanked her for the lift. As she drove off I was relieved to see a bus coming in the opposite direction. This got me back to school a little quicker than expected, but my hopes of escaping discreetly from the building were dashed when I noticed that I was boxed in by two cars, one of which I recognised as being owned by a teacher I knew well. He was also the type who would make a public meal out of my stupidity! Anyway, I had no choice but to brave the bear pit of the staffroom and hope that either most of the teachers had left, or that no one there had noticed that I had already left the premises earlier.

My arrival in the staffroom started OK as I even fibbed about doing some marking before going home as being the reason for my continued presence in school, but when I sheepishly asked my friend to move his car he commented after a puzzled frown, 'But I saw you going home in Jackie's car about forty minutes ago!' The pause that followed from me, coupled with previous examples of my absent mindedness was sufficient for him to realise the truth and within a few minutes I was the subject of much ridicule and mirth from the ten or so teachers present. However, I subsequently managed to get home just in time to fulfil my chauffeuring duties.

This incident was worrying enough by itself, but the following week I did it again! On this occasion I even got as far as my house before I noticed that my wife was at home but the car wasn't. My embarrassment was so acute that I vowed to tell no one, provided I could sneak back onto the school site without anyone noticing. I managed this by using a circuitous route around the buildings, with extra cover provided by some mature trees. To my joy I was not boxed in and managed to make good my escape.

After a steadying cup of tea at home the evening's conversation developed into the likelihood that I was developing the early signs of Alzheimer's, but it soon became evident that I had always had a tendency to be thinking of other things when even basic concentration on the moment at hand would have 'saved' me. My wife reminded me of the times I had either missed my stop on the train home from work or left something on the luggage rack, when I had endured a brief period of work as an admin clerk at County Hall in London. At the time I had put this down to the tedious nature of the work, coupled with the crush and boredom of the rail journey, making me into a temporary zombie, but perhaps I am just absent minded. My close friends are in no doubt!

Postscript: It seems it was my turn to appear on the 'Meet the teacher' page of the school magazine the following week, which my friend (boxed-in car) unfortunately edited. I was interviewed by a very keen year seven student and the results included;

Favourite singer: Elvis Presley
Interests: drawing, reading, golf and hiking
Favourite book: *Birdsong*
Favourite TV programmes: any history or nature
Favourite film: *Dude, Where's my Car?...* which I still haven't seen!

Absent minded...take two

As I walked into the secretaries' office with some typing I was hoping to charm them into doing (I didn't), one of the secretaries, Diana, called me over and said she was in the process of updating all the teachers' qualifications for the new school brochure, the final page of which always had a list (in order of seniority) of the staff and their academic achievements. Mine were quite modest so I always used to ask Diana to introduce a few extra spaces on my line to give the appearance that there were more than I actually had. However, on this occasion she was ready for me and after telling not to bother asking for the usual 'spacing', handed me a piece of paper and asked me to jot down an up-to-date list of my qualifications.

I was reassured on looking at the entries made by one or two new members of staff which were not too long or impressive and proceeded to jot down my list, which included a BA, a couple of diplomas and the usual teacher's certificate. After a moment's thought to see if I had forgotten anything, I added one more qualification, which resulted in my line stretching out just a little further than at least one senior member of staff. 'Never mind the quality, feel the width,' passed my mind as I left the room following a final attempt to get my typing done, which failed due to the appearance of a boy with a grazed knee and a couple of his friends who were demanding action against an older boy who had pushed him over.

It was a few days later that I read a copy of the brochure during the lunch break. I quickly scanned through the usual 'promotional sections', took a little longer over the exam results, but was really interested in getting to the teacher's qualifications, both to see who the latest 'superstars' were to join the staff, but also to see where I stood in the pecking order of qualifications...It was only then that I realised what I had done a few days earlier! I rushed down to see Diana who thankfully was alone and quickly asked her if the brochure was the final copy. The conversation went something like this...

Diana: 'Yes, I always leave a few spares in the staff room for the teachers.'

PF: 'But I wrote down something on my qualifications which wasn't true!'

Diana: 'What do you mean...Why?'

PF: 'I just did it for a joke. When I handed it to you I was sure you would ask me straight away about one of my qualifications. Then I must have been distracted and forgot about it.'

Diana, looking at the relevant page: 'What's the problem, haven't you got a BA?'

PF: 'Yes, but...'

Diana: 'And a teacher's certificate?'

PF: 'Yes.'

Diana: 'And...'

PF, interrupting: 'Diana, it's the last one!'

Diana, reading, looking puzzled: 'I don't understand. What is this qualification you've got, an "HBL"?'

PF, reluctantly: 'A Hunk of Burning Love.'

There followed a momentary pause during which I wasn't sure if Diana was going to kill me or laugh. Being Diana, she managed both and as she had no wish to either 'explain' the error to the headmaster, or reprint the whole brochure, we agreed to leave things as they were unless the topic was raised by another member of staff, in which case I was to either come clean or create a qualification to match the offending letters. I never got further than 'Higher, or Honorary' something or other. Amazingly, the entry went unnoticed for the whole year and the truth was only revealed many years later at a gathering of teacher friends when we all had to confess to something illegal that we had done.

Being a 'goody goody' I had nothing to offer, but after much pressure came up with this true story.

Cover lesson

I remember as a fairly recently qualified teacher (a long time ago) how annoying it was to be given a cover lesson when all you really wanted to spend your free time on is preparing the next lesson, recovering from the last one, or just sleeping. So I did feel slightly sorry for one NQT (newly qualified teacher) when he looked at the cover list one morning and found himself 'covering' a rather unruly year nine set for a teacher struck down with the flu. I did, however, give him the directions required to find the classroom before he trudged off rather disconsolately towards his first lesson, to be followed by the dreaded cover.

My morning went surprisingly well and by the time the morning break bell sounded I was in the mood for a bit of mischief in the staffroom.

My mood was further lightened by not only being first in the queue for coffee and goodies but also noticing that bread pudding (one of my favourites … is food a recurring theme in this book?) was on the menu.

I sat down and shared a few jokes with some chums, one of whom also told me that a disruptive student I should have been taking had just been excluded for at least a week (yippee – two lessons!).

A few moments later a rather worried NQT came in and sat next to me. I asked if anything was wrong and he firstly looked around and then, satisfied that no one was listening, proceeded to tell me how he had gone to the cover classroom about five minutes before the lesson was due to start, but no one had turned up even after ten minutes.

He thought at first that he had gone to the wrong room and, therefore, rushed back to the staffroom to check that he had the correct time and place.

On confirming that this was correct he decided to just stay in the room and continue with a lesson plan he had started earlier.

He was really worried about doing something wrong!

I actually knew that the whole year group had been asked to attend an 'emergency' assembly as an undesirable and unknown adult had been seen on the school premises on more than one occasion that week, but my childish sense of humour got the better of me, so in response to his plea 'I hope I haven't done anything wrong,' I replied, 'No, not at all ... I'm surprised no one explained the cover system to you! You see, if it's your first ever cover, the teacher in charge of cover just gives you an empty classroom. If you look after the room and leave it tidy then you get some pupils second time!'

I fully expected this bit of nonsense to be exposed instantly for the silly joke that it was, but what I didn't know was that this poor teacher had not only had a difficult week, but had also had a few too many drinks at the new staff welcome event the previous evening.

He did look a little puzzled, but a quick look at my very serious face, plus his relief at not having made a mistake encouraged him to take my explanation at face value.

I was only going to let him suffer for a few minutes, but I was suddenly called to the phone with a request from a parent.

As I replaced the phone I realised to my embarrassment that he was now explaining the cover system to a couple of friends of his, both also NQTs. They looked momentarily puzzled before asking who had passed on this information. As soon as he pointed in my direction and said my name I couldn't keep a straight face and they both burst out laughing! I immediately apologised and also told a fib about how the same trick had been played on me as an NQT.

This just about saved me and I also added later in private that he would never have fallen for such a silly joke if he hadn't been feeling a little the worse for wear. To his credit he saw the funny side of things almost immediately ... little did I know that revenge would be very sweet a few weeks later.

Revenge

I found myself once again in a pretty good mood in the staffroom at lunch. It was my birthday and I was being treated to one of my wife's favourite recipes that evening, followed by a trip to the cinema. The only cloud on the horizon was a school football match the following evening, Friday.

This was the one night that most P.E. teachers did not want to do 'extra time', not only because it was the end of a long and tiring week, but there was also the prospect of Saturday morning football to further eat into the idea of a 'free' weekend. It was also a long minibus journey into London to play against a grammar school who always gave us a good thrashing! (Although we were situated in the London Borough of Bromley we were obliged to travel long distances on at least five or six occasions a season to play 'historical' fixtures against grammar or ex-grammar schools; we were of the ex variety.)

The weather, however, held out some hope! It had been raining non-stop for about three days, a fact that would not affect the Saturday matches on our field, but could well mean the end for the Friday game on the low lying and notoriously badly drained grammar school pitch.

My hopes had been further raised by two members of the P.E. department, Gary and Malcolm, who had expressed their belief that I would be receiving a phone call sometime today with the joyous news that the match was off!

About halfway through the lunch break one of the school secretaries brought a note asking me to phone a Mr C Lion about Friday's football at the Regents Park number written down.

I was so excited at the prospect of the match being cancelled that I didn't even stop to wonder why a teacher from Dulwich would be phoning me from central London.

I dialled the number and instead of a school switch-board or P.E. teacher, received the words, 'Hallo, London Zoo here, how can I help you?'

As the terrible truth dawned upon my very gullible self I began to turn round in the vain hope that the individual who had played the practical joke on me was not actually in the staffroom. (I could deal with the secretary later.)

I was greeted by a sudden burst of applause from about ten teachers who were 'in' on the plot, three of whom had also quickly donned some animal masks

and were making the appropriate noises ... but the final insult was delivered by the aforementioned NQT who not only handed me a slip showing that I had been given a cover later on in the day, but also informed me that it was a pretty rough class!

Retirement Assistance

As I approached retirement age I started to receive some unusual junk mail in my 'pigeon hole' at school. Someone was having an age joke at my expense by regularly providing me with useful information about cheap travel offers for senior citizens, or special bingo days for the elderly in our area and also information on the most up to date 'Batricars', stairlifts, or Zimmer frames etc.

I was actually quite impressed with the efforts of the mystery prankster as he or she had even managed to enrol me onto one or two courses without me knowing anything about them (I actually went on the 'Preparation for Retirement' day which was quite informative) and had even subscribed on my behalf to a number of 'senior' magazines, including *Saga* and one or two quite snappily-titled numbers concerned with diet and exercise for the elderly.

I had some strong suspicions as to who the culprit might be, but he had either improved his acting considerably, or was innocent.

At the end of my final Christmas term we had the usual staff drink in the staffroom before everyone either went home or made their way to one of the local pubs.

I couldn't understand why so many people were giving me hearty slaps on the back and telling me how

PETER FOSTER

much I was going to be missed. After all I still had six months to go! As the party wore on I began to wonder why there was so much giggling going on, coupled with an unusual number of staff staring in my direction.

I checked my trouser zip but all was OK. A quick glance into a mirror also revealed no facial blemishes, so what was going on and what did my chum Matt mean when he suggested I should go to the toilet as I was looking 'a little full'? I had deliberately only had one lager shandy as it was going to be a long night at the pub!

I eventually found out that all the friendly backslapping was in fact a cover and that a colostomy bag complete with yellow liquid (orange juice) had been attached to my back!

As my last day at school got even closer the frequency of the 'useful information' stepped up to an even higher level and on one day I was asked to collect a large package from the site manager's office.

It was a very large cardboard box and as I began to open it I thought this might be a special retirement present that had just arrived a little early. For a moment I even considered asking a few of my friends if I shouldn't open it until the last day … but curiosity got the better of me and I decided to have a look inside. What I found however, was another slightly smaller box, which led me to think that I was about to suffer the 'Russian doll' gag, where you open numerous packages of ever-decreasing size to eventually arrive at a very small and insignificant 'present'.

But as I began to peel away the second layer of cardboard my hopes were raised by the sight of a shiny metal bar. Could it be a new golf trolley? Or even better a new set of irons?

I frantically ripped away some more bits of cardboard and within a few minutes the identity of the present was revealed – a shiny new Zimmer frame with a note attached to it. 'Please return the frame to Bromley Hospital when you have finished using it'!

My good friend Matt eventually owned up to being the sender of my retirement 'help' and as well as buying him a well earned drink, I was also able to use his 'jokes' as material for my leaving speech.

School Assembly

Being ex-grammar, my final school still clung on to many of its old traditions. Thus, in the 1980s the school assembly was still very much a reflection on what had gone on over half a century before. Some piano music would accompany the various classes and teachers as they entered the hall; the senior staff would all sit on the stage in their academic gowns and the assembly itself was usually a combination of a religious reading followed by a hymn and any relevant notices that had to be read out to the school.

Just occasionally, there would be some additions, which could include the announcement of some sporting successes or perhaps a musical item from a talented pupil. These did break the tedium to some extent, but a glance around the hall inevitably revealed a number of bored or semi-sleeping students probably wishing they were still in bed!

The head of music at the time, Paul, was the best piano player, so it fell to him to play the introductory music. This actually annoyed him somewhat as not being a form tutor he would otherwise be free to either relax or prepare for the day's first lesson. Indeed, on more than one occasion he had asked to be relieved of piano playing duties, or at least be part of a rota, as there were at least another two competent piano players amongst the staff.

Unfortunately, the headmaster viewed the situation differently and saw it as part of the head of music's brief to play the piano at assembly. It would be an exaggeration to say that this duty spoiled Paul's day, but it was probably advisable to talk to him after assembly!

After about ten years at the school, he decided it was time to move on and he was successful in an interview for head of music at a prestigious private London school. This was also an opportunity for him to fulfil a career ambition in 'directing' the school choir who performed regularly at the local (famous) church.

I was sorry to see him leave as he had been responsible for not only running an excellent department, but also organising and directing some wonderful musical events, including the Christmas concert and the music for various school plays.

It was a few days before he was due to leave and as we were good friends I had promised to make time to sit down with him and indulge in a few reminiscences, as well as wishing him all the best for the future. My opportunity came one break when I spotted him alone in the staffroom. After a few laughs over old incidents and a brief discussion about his new school, he announced, 'and I won't have to play at assemblies at the new school!' We had a laugh about this and just as I was about to leave he said, 'And I've chosen a special piece of music for my last assembly.' Giving this no more thought I took myself off to the pleasures of 3B history.

On Paul's last day he was in position at the front of the hall as usual, waiting for the procession of senior teachers resplendent in their academic gowns to make their way down the hall's centre isle to the stage. The headteacher at the time was admirably brisk in everything he did and always marched up to the stage at such a speed that his academic gown flowed out, cape-like, behind him.

The stage was set, with senior staff making final adjustments to their gowns in a small entrance hall just outside the main hall. The head was always particularly careful to make sure the back of his gown wasn't caught in anything.

On this morning I was on door duty, which meant that as soon as all the relevant 'VIPs' were ready I could go into the hall and raise an arm to Paul to indicate that it was time for him to start playing.

All was ready, so I asked the two door prefects to open the doors. The hall fell silent and Paul raised his hands a little more theatrically than usual before beginning to play a deliberately slow and 'classical' version of 'The Darth Vader Theme' from *Star Wars* as the head's 'cape' flowed majestically out behind him!

It took a moment or two before most of the teachers present realised the significance of the music as Paul was phrasing the tune to create a suitably dramatic moment, but eventually I was forced to join in a stifled giggle.

The pupils, however, latched on much quicker and many were chuckling away quietly as the procession continued.

As the headmaster reached the stage he seemed a little puzzled by this slight disturbance in the ranks, but his mind must have been on the assembly, which included one or two serious announcements.

One of his stares, combined with an intake of breath and thrusting chest, was sufficient to establish order and the assembly soon returned to normal.

I expected Paul to be summoned to the head's office later in the day, but he 'escaped'. Whether the head had not recognised the music or had just decided not to take Paul to task on his last day, no one really knows. But Paul couldn't resist a sly wink in my direction as he left the hall for the final time!

Storms and Snow

Much as I loved my job it was really nice to have the occasional unexpected day (or days) off.

The first of these 'opportunities' was during my two-year stint at a very tough inner city London school in the early '70s when a national strike meant that the premises was rapidly running out of its oil (heating) supply.

The subject dominated staff meetings for at least a couple of weeks, but as none of the staff wished to be viewed as 'skivers' the information was very much one way (from the headmaster to us) without too many enquiries as to the likelihood of the school closing.

And then one afternoon a message was sent round to teachers announcing a short but important staff meeting that evening.

This was it! We were closing the school and with no end to the dispute in sight, who knew for how long!

That afternoon I started to plan for this period of 'leave'.

I decided to be a good boy for at least half of every day, by preparing future lessons meticulously and even catching up with all my marking. But the idea of not having to travel from south east London to south west and return, coupled with some relaxation time was beginning to dominate my thoughts.

As I entered the staff room that evening there was an unusual state of animation amongst the teachers, most of whom had been discussing the various options open to the head and the local authorities for a large part of the afternoon.

Imagine our disappointment when we were informed that as the heating oil was due to run out by the end of the week, the pupils were to be told to stay away from school for health and safety reasons as it was December and the forecast was for a cold spell. The teachers, however, were to attend unless the temperature in the building dropped to a certain unacceptable level.

Horrors! A long journey to a freezing old Victorian school while the kids had free time.

That evening I had the occasional thought of revenge.

I would set an unreasonable amount of homework at a really tough level with severe punishment for any pupil who did not complete it perfectly! Eventually, however, reason won and I was resigned to my fate.

Some of my colleagues later admitted to considering either tampering with the wall thermometer that was to be responsible for either keeping everyone at school or giving us freedom, or increasing the cold air around it by 'tweeking' some of the doors and windows in the immediate area to introduce a cold draught. Two brave souls had even had the guts to ask the head to allow those who wished to stay at home provided they provided proof that they were 'working'. Another suggested that as teachers we should be trusted to work at home and that in this circumstance the travel to and from school was just a waste of time.

This was not acceptable to the local authority, however, as the head subsequently informed us, so our only hope was for the predicted cold spell to be so severe that the school would have to close.

It is fair to say that for the next three evenings I showed an interest in the weather forecast that had not previously been evident.

Yes, it was getting colder, but not cold enough!

And so for the next few school days, the staff of our cold and strangely quiet school sat huddled around a few electric fires in the staffroom, doing their best to continue working.

And then it got really cold. Minus five and snow threatening!

To our credit on the day after the drop in temperature (a Friday) the staff were still to be seen working diligently in their winter woollies, although there were many, and frequent, visits to check the thermometer!

And then our wonderful headmaster entered the staffroom and informed us that as the temperature in the building was below the accepted level we were being instructed to work from home until further notice.

There was a rapid packing of books etc. followed by a few more kisses and hugs than was usual on a Friday evening, plus some very conscientious exchanging of phone numbers between members of departments, before the school emptied and closed for what turned out to be two weeks.

My next memory of severe weather affecting work was in 1978. We had only just moved from south east London to Biggin Hill in north Kent. Our house was in a valley, which was notoriously difficult to get out of in a car if the snow was too severe for the road gritters, or they had just simply not done their job correctly!

That year the snow was really heavy for a few weeks. So much so in fact that at the top of our valley (one of the highest spots on the North Downs) the snow, aided by some strong winds, had caused such severe drifting that half of a fairly busy road had been covered up to the height of the top of a bus stop!

I felt a bit like Scott or Shackleton as I trudged my way up the hill each morning to hopefully catch a bus into Bromley in time for school. I had made it on every day for the first week of the 'blizzard', but as I looked out of my bedroom window early on the following Monday morning I realised there had been a really heavy fall overnight and it had been very windy. Would the bus still be running?

I set off a little earlier than usual with a hot flask of coffee, some snacks and a change of underwear in case I was snowed in for the night far from home (I had friends who lived near our school, so I didn't have to freeze to death!) and was soon knee-deep in fresh and drifting snow. Halfway up the hill to the bus stop I bumped in to some familiar faces from my usual bus who informed me that they had not seen a bus despite arriving at the stop an hour earlier than usual. I could have gone home but the spirit of adventure had caught hold of me and I decided to trudge the six miles, mostly downhill, to Bromley.

At first the going was very slow due to drifting on top of the Downs. But I knew that only a mile or so further on the road had been cleared only a few days earlier and therefore, the snow was likely to be less deep. And so it was. I was on a strenuous, but strangely exciting trek to my destination. My high spirits probably also had something to do with my always enjoying a change from normal routine. This was becoming much more fun than a smoky, sweaty, thirty minutes in a bus and the school day could possibly also be a rearranged one due to staff shortages. Visions of films in the school hall and groups enjoying extra P.E. lessons spurred me on. I also became more and more in tune with nature as I passed through an area with a beautiful display of hoar frost on tree branches.

I probably took twice as long as it would normally take me to walk the six miles, but as I turned into school I was in a good mood, especially as I would almost certainly be congratulated by the headmaster for my 'dedication to the cause'. I was, however, slightly disappointed by the sparcity of cars in the car park. Some teachers lived less than a mile from the school! Still, maybe they had walked. There also seemed to be very few students around. A slide in the top playground was being used by about ten boys and one or two were throwing snowballs in the lower.

I entered the school and decided to go straight to the headmaster's office to both modestly accept praise for my epic journey and also to receive instructions as to my 'role' for the day.

I knocked on the door and was welcomed in by a rather surprised headmaster. I told him that as there were no buses I had walked to school and apologised for being late. He replied, 'Don't apologise, Peter, I can only commend you for taking the trouble to walk all this way. Unfortunately I closed the school about an hour ago as only two teachers had been able to get in! Would you like a cup of coffee before you go home? I would offer you some food but none of the cooks have arrived!'

I did have a coffee before trudging back through even deeper snow and a bitingly cold wind ... a journey taking an extra hour due to the fact that it was uphill, and my aching legs and sagging spirits were really slowing me down!

The next day due to mounting criticism from the local media and public, the gritters were out early and the bus was running!

The most dramatic weather event that occurred during my teaching career has to be the Great Storm of 1987!

I remember being up for most of the night with my wife and children, watching and listening to the huge winds that battered our part of the North Downs. It was impossible to sleep as we heard trees and branches falling; in addition, some electricity cables became loose and we watched with fascination and fear as one or two of them snaked up and down the street giving off quite dramatic sparks in the process.

In the early hours there was a thirty-minute power cut and then the wind seemed to ease a little so we tried to grab some sleep.

The morning revealed a large tree at the end of our garden had fallen down and was lying right across our neighbours' garden. When I spoke to 'the man of the house' he wasn't at all worried and informed me that the tree should have been in his garden anyway, but the previous occupants of our house had built a new fence around it on the wrong side! He proceeded to calmly saw it up for firewood over the next few weeks, whenever he needed to replenish his stock and by the end of the winter it was all gone.

I had decided to go to school in my walking gear as I fully expected at least one tree to be blocking the bus route. In fact there were many and I had to walk over four miles before finding a bus route still open.

On the way I managed to help with moving some smaller branches from four blocked road sections and it was almost a disappointment when a bus came along. I only had a few miles to go, but as I sat down a lack of sleep and the effects of all my physical exertions were beginning to take their toll…

I was rudely awakened by an elderly lady who prodded me on the shoulders and then said, 'Aren't you going to help young fellow?'

She was pointing to a tree in front of the bus that was already being attacked by a tree surgeon.

I got off the bus and sleepily started moving some of the logs to a stack by the side of the road, making a mental note to inform a friend (with a woodburner) where this stash of gold was situated.

It was when I looked up that I realised I was three miles past my school! I was understandably late due to the storm, but now even further late due to having fallen asleep!

I rushed across the road to the nearest bus stop in the other direction, but then waited for over half an hour for a bus. I had already phoned the school to warn them that I may be late due to road blockages forcing me to walk, but was still keen to get to school as quickly as possible.

The bus had just pulled out when a police car swung in front of us blocking the road. An officer got out and informed our driver that a large and unsafe tree was on our route and it would have to be cut down before the route could be declared 'safe'. I asked him how long this was likely to be and he solemnly advised all on the bus that it would be at least three hours.

I had no alternative but to walk again and eventually arrived at school at lunchtime, which would have been fine if the cooks had turned up!

There were some students in classrooms, the caretaker was clearing away some branches from trees on the school field, so I had hopes that my trip had not been in vain.

A colleague shouted out to me from the staffroom window that I wasn't dressed properly, but then kindly informed me that there was a rota of teaching duties in the staffroom as so many staff and children had not turned up.

My name had been put down for a film in the hall, which the whole of the lower school were going to watch and then library duty with two classes crammed into the upper school section.

This was OK, but then I caught sight of another notice that due to the non arrival of a teacher I was to cover that person's detention duty!

It was the end of a far from perfect day when after more walking I arrived home in the dark, only to listen to stories of a fun time from my gleeful children whose school had been closed for the day due to staff absences!

A New Species?

It was lunch duty on a beautiful summer's day.

In the winter, drawing the 'short straw' meant a cold playground plus the occasional trek up to the school playing field to see if any smokers were lighting up; but in the summer the duty became a pleasant breath of fresh air often coupled with some light conversation with both fellow members of staff who were on duty and pupils who sometimes liked to come over and have a chat.

On this occasion, the warm weather had created a relaxed atmosphere and after two slow laps of the field I settled down on a bench under a tree to both observe proceedings while at the same time, rest my aching legs after the rigours of joining in a 1,500metres that morning.

Within a few minutes a few pupils from my previous lesson had gathered round for a 'parlez' and the conversation moved from the weather, through which of the lady teachers I thought was the best looking (I was very professional and diplomatic) and then on to what everyone was going to do that weekend.

There were three boys and two girls from year ten present and the conversations ranged through a number of events including parties, swimming clubs and 'going to my mate's'. One boy even admitted he was going to do some homework!

Eventually the conversation got round to me, but before I could answer, one of the lads chipped in by announcing that my weekend would obviously consist of marking and preparation, plus three early nights to prepare me for the rigours of the following week.

I waited for a few moments expecting one of the others to point out that I may actually have a life away from school, but no one was forthcoming, so I proceeded to surprise everyone by going through my plans, which that weekend included a party with some friends, a round of golf and a trip to Hever Castle for a medieval jousting tournament with the family.

They all seemed quite surprised at these revelations and proceeded to ask me about a number of the other teachers' hobbies, family etc. I couldn't go into too much personal detail and resisted questions about which teacher was going out with who, but as the end of lunch bell rang I hopefully had changed a few opinions about teachers.

In fact, as they walked away one of the girls turned round and thanked me for the conversation, ending with the comment, 'You know, Sir, I had no idea that teachers did all those normal things in their spare time … some of you must be almost human!'

Pupil Power

The 1970s, following the Swinging 60s, was a decade of protest against war, capitalism and many other things! I even had long hair, my beard had grown unkempt and at the weekends I could be seen in sandals and cheesecloth shirts! On the music front I was still faithful to Elvis when he was in the recording studio, but found his films embarrassing and the soundtracks (with a few exceptions) generally poor. I had, however, branched out into the folk movement and had the LPs to prove it. There was even a rumour that I was spotted dancing naked in the rain at the Norfolk Folk Festival!

At Quernmore School, these changes were only noticeable amongst the pupils in hairstyles and the occasional attempt to rebel by introducing some clothing that broke the school rules, or by just being a little scruffier than usual. The sixth form boys, however, had become a little more militant and after a series of meetings with the senior staff and backing from certain parents, they had managed to bring about some minor changes to the sixth form clothing, were allowed to leave school when they didn't have a lesson and perhaps most significantly had been allocated their own common room.

The common room question had been on the school agenda for a number of years. Recently, however, the mood of refusal had been softening as the school was keen to hang on to its brightest sixth form members, who, due to an education department initiative, could now move to another school in the borough if the courses or facilities caught their eye.

And so it was that a number of sixth formers were now to be found in a small room quite close to the staffroom.

This, in itself, caused some friction amongst the staff, some of whom resented students, albeit senior ones, in such close proximity.

They were worried that their peace at breaktime would be shattered by Bob Dylan belting out 'The Times They are a Changing' from the allocated record player and also that staff privacy would be compromised.

In fact, the staff became quite split in their opinions about the common room, with some complaining about the noise, others about the mess and a few also pointed out that the furniture provided for the lads was being treated badly. Others defended the sixth formers right to have their own space and one brave soul even pointed out that the staff had no right to complain as the sink area in the staffroom was constantly left in a mess with unwashed plates and cups and a fridge that needed a serious sort out and clean due to food and milk etc. being left there for a lot longer than its 'use by' date.

One senior (in years and service) member of staff was particularly annoyed at this pandering to the sixth form. 'We didn't have this or that when I was in the sixth form!' was a common loud phrase to be heard in the staffroom. He would then go on to describe the spartan conditions in his boarding school, including freezing dormitories and rock-hard chairs. In addition, he regularly used to fling open the door of the common room to hopefully catch some of the boys 'up to no good'.

He was not only unsuccessful in his attempts, but also annoyed the sixth form who regularly raised the subject of these 'intrusions into their privacy' at the monthly school council. Luckily for them, the headmaster was on their side and despite a few polite requests from him with regard to cleanliness and noise, the common room had become a permanent institution.

It was one day in the spring of '75 (sounds like a protest song title) when matters reached a climax!

The 'anti-common room' senior member of staff was sitting opposite me moaning to anyone who may be listening about the latest 'soft' concession to the sixth form, which was the purchase of a pool table and dartboard for the boys' use. Whereas the noise from the common room was always fairly loud it was now also regularly punctuated by shouts of delight as a difficult black was potted or a treble twenty hit.

He tried to calm himself by opening the sports page of *The Times*, but was soon ruffling it in an agitated state and mumbling something about 'spoilt kids'. As another cheer burst forth he could stand it no more, so he jumped up and rushed out of the room. I followed fearing a bloodbath and found him hovering for a second in the hallway outside the common room. Deciding that it was the moment to strike he threw the door open and strode inside. I then heard a muffled scream and boys gasping!

Fearing violence, I rushed along the corridor to see him shaking in the doorway with his back turned to me. As he turned round I noticed he had a dart in his ear and behind him was the thrower still holding an impressive follow through position with his right arm!

It was, of course an accident and rather than face the humiliation of explaining what had happened to another teacher or emergency department at the local hospital, he requested a plaster, on receipt of which he manfully pulled out the dart (which he later destroyed) and attached the plaster to his slightly-bleeding ear. I assisted him for a few minutes and even considered mentioning that he wouldn't need to pay for an ear piercing now, but a look at his face revealed considerable anger and humiliation and I was just grateful that he agreed to go back to the staffroom.

The headmaster was very sympathetic about this injury but after interviewing some witnesses, including yours truly, refused to follow up the charge of attempted murder and settled instead for an insistence that the dartboard be repositioned to a less dangerous corner of the room.

The sixth-form common room was respectfully quieter for a few days and the boy who threw the dart attempted to apologise to the injured party without much success!

Inter-School Staff Cricket

From time to time the P.E. staff from one school would challenge another to some sort of match on a Friday evening.

This was meant to be a social event where, after the sport the participants all gathered at a nearby pub to socialise.

Inevitably, however, (and particularly amongst the men) the desire to win regularly filtered into the proceedings, especially if someone had a reputation as a good player in that sport to uphold.

So these events sometimes got a bit 'silly'! At one stage there was even a league table between two schools and a regular series of matches between these two often became quite heated despite the façade of the event just being 'a bit of fun'. Behind the organisation of these events was an element of showing off and one-upmanship!

This was not the case, however, between our school and one of our closest neighbours. When we joined together for the occasional Friday evening the accent was very much on fun and if anyone wasn't particularly good at a particular sport they were not humiliated, but encouraged by perhaps receiving a softer forehand at tennis, or a deliberately easy catch at cricket, as well as some useful coaching points.

On one particularly lovely summer's evening it was our turn to stage a cricket match.

The two worst players were chosen as captains, the ball that exploded into a puff of powder carefully hidden away and the umpire informed that he was to give the best batsman out for a stumping with a second ball hidden in the wicketkeeper's pads! The double-headed coin was tossed and their first two batsmen began to pad up.

Despite our best intentions, the opposition were bowled out for a modest seventy-five runs, despite us allowing two people who were out to return to the crease and a couple of 'sitter catches' to deliberately fall from the hands.

Being our best batsman by a mile with a county captaincy and tour of Australia to boot, Gary was often placed well down the batting order, but having not needed to bat for a couple of innings it was felt that he deserved a knock and so he and another fairly competent player were the openers.

I was batting number ten and felt so confident in our line up that I suggested a set or two of tennis with a colleague (batting eleven) to while away an hour or so before we would be needed to bat.(Gary would probably score at least fifty before deliberately giving a catch.)

As we strolled up to the tennis courts I turned to see Gary stroke a superb four to midwicket before turning my thoughts to my troubled service action!

After a few games it was clear that John, a younger and more powerful player than me, was in a relaxed state of mind and had decided to allow the match to be quite close. My serve was also working better than usual, so the first set score was a creditable 7–5 to John and I was actually leading 3–1 in the second when John had to go outside the court to fetch a ball he had sliced over the fence in a vain attempt to control one of my vicious serves (it actually was harder than usual). The cricket pitch was hidden from the tennis courts by some trees and a few minutes earlier we had both commented that the cheers and shouts from the pavilion had gone strangely quiet. After picking up the ball he turned towards the cricketers, scratched his head and then jogged back to the court.

I asked him if anything was wrong and he told me that all the players seemed to have gone!

We both found this a little puzzling as we had calculated that even if Gary had decided to let rip, we would still have plenty of time for at least a couple of sets ...we decided to go and investigate.

As I turned the corner by the pavilion, only Gary was present and in the distance I could see the teachers from our neighbouring school getting into their minibus.

I apologised for not being present to watch him score the winning run and also for not 'saying goodbye' to the other members of staff. He remained strangely quiet, so I asked him what was wrong. He replied, 'Pete, I haven't scored the winning run, I was out some time ago. So were all of the others. In fact we were struggling! When it was your turn to go in, no one had a clue where you were. We looked in the school and the staffroom and other places, but after about ten minutes the other team and quite a few of ours were so fed up they just decided to leave, which was a pity because the score was getting quite interesting; we only needed ten to win!'

I was mortified! An otherwise enjoyable evening had been spoilt by my unexplained absence!

I asked Gary why he didn't check the tennis courts and secretly cursed myself for not saying where we were. I even thought about admonishing Gary for not thinking to check the tennis courts, but a look at his angry face made me ditch this idea.

Still, all was not lost. I quickly shouted to Gary that I was going to get their players back. 'It doesn't matter about the rest of our team, it's only me and John left to bat!'

I dashed off to the car park and was just in time to leap out in front of the minibus and stop it! I went round to the driver and, out of breath, explained my mistake, apologised and pleaded with the team to come back and finish the match.

The driver turned round to some stern faces, who all shook their heads in the negative.

'I'm not sure if we will be seeing you again on a Friday, goodnight!' were his final words as he smartly drove off and I was left alone with the knowledge that I had not only spoilt the event, but was probably the sole cause of it being the last of its kind.

I tried one more shout, complete with pleading arms, but it was no good. They were off and my name was muck!

I strolled back up to the pavilion and sat head in hands while Gary completed his packing and locking away of the cricket bags.

I told him, once again, how sorry I was but he just ignored me. A few minutes later he was ready to leave and I was contemplating the reception I would receive in the staffroom on Monday when Gary usually announced the staff match results and thanked everyone who took part!

He walked away from me and then suddenly turned and stopped, saying, 'You might at least ask me how many runs I scored!' Seeing this as a chance to get him to speak to me again, I did. He replied, 'Well, you know they scored seventy-five – it was all over quite quickly. We won seventy-six for one and I was not out fifty-two.'

All the players had been in on the wind-up of course and I received a great cheer from everyone as the pub door swung open!

The Great Fire of Bromley

Ihave been responsible for a number of misjudgements during my teaching career (not too many!), but this incident is probably the worst. I hope that as it took place many years ago I will not be prosecuted and that all my colleagues who only heard the partial truth (due more to embarrassment than a desire to conceal the facts) will forgive me. Here, the true story is revealed!

It was a fairly run-of-the-mill day at school with my lessons being unremarkable with regard to both content and incident. I had given a detention in a geography lesson to a boy who had failed to provide homework for the third week running, but felt that this was justified as he had had fair warning and there were no problems at home etc. I had also received parental support for my action through a recent phone call. (I actually prided myself with issuing relatively few 'DTs' – a reflection, no doubt, on my superb pupil control and wonderfully interesting lessons.) I was, however, getting a little tired as midday approached, due to a half round of golf played before school with three fellow teacher friends, a regular weekly event which I really enjoyed as it definitely made me feel much more alert by the time I arrived at school, especially if I had played well.

This morning had been particularly enjoyable because I had not only won, but also cracked a few of my corny jokes which seemed to go down well with my playing partners...When John had asked me how I 'found' the greens on the course, I dredged up the age-old 'Well, if you walk down the fairway, there they are right in front of you,' and my attempt to help improve Steve's bunker play with 'Imagine the ball is a fried egg and try to hit the white and follow through' (which is actually quite good advice) encouraged a whole range of culinary references for the next half hour or so. For example, when I asked Steve how I should negotiate a tree directly in line with the pin he suggested I 'Give it a banana round the left side' whereas his own attempt to get out of the woods at the next hole which hit a succession of trees and changed direction at least three times was described as 'A bit of a spaghetti' by John.

The problem with early morning golf was that it left me a bit tired by about midday, a feeling compounded by the thirty-degree temperature on this particular glorious summer day.

Still, as I climbed the stairs towards 1B geography I had a feeling that all was well with the world. A glance through a window confirmed that I would be able to top up my sun tan at home for a couple of hours after school and within ten minutes peace had descended on the classroom as the boys attempted their end of term assessment paper. I actually found tests fairly boring but after the exertions of morning golf it was nice to let my mind drift towards the glories of my 'birdie' at the sixth and the perfectly straight drive down the ninth, despite Steve's attempt to influence matters with a reference to the fact that I had hit a tree the previous week.

I was only really disturbed by the noise from some builders who had been repairing the gutters and fascias around the roof all week, but even the drill and sawing noises stopped after about twenty minutes and soon I was fighting a strong desire to close my eyes.

I must have dropped off for a few seconds when a cough from somewhere in the room jolted me back into the world and the sight of three hands up in the air. I decided to deal with Harry's problem first, moved over to his desk and asked him how I could help. He was having difficulty remembering how to work out a grid reference on the ordinance survey question, having forgotten if it was the vertical or horizontal number first. I quietly told him that I couldn't help him, but relented slightly when the second questioner had the same problem. Perhaps I hadn't taught this well enough? Being in a benevolent frame of mind and having checked that a few more puzzled frowns were working on the same question, I stopped the test for a moment and announced that I was going to give everyone a reminder about question fourteen. This was in the form of a clue about which number came first in the form of the phrase 'You go along the corridor and then up the stairs.' Despite one or two blank faces there was a general sigh of recognition and calm was restored, except for a usually meek young man who still had his hand sheepishly half raised. I was quite surprised as he was the type who would rather get a question wrong than make a fuss, but put on a reassuring smile as I worked my way over to his desk. I asked how I could help but barely heard his response. Asking him to speak up a little he repeated, 'Sir, I think I can smell some smoke.' My sense of smell has always been terrible due to an unknown nasal allergy regularly blocking my sinuses, so after a couple of sniffs I had a quick look round the room and out of the window, where the workmens' scaffolding was empty, possibly due to them deciding to take an early lunch break. I couldn't see any problem either in or outside the room and after a reassuring word to the boy began to move back to my desk. I was stopped, however, by another pupil who told me he could not only smell smoke but could see some coming through a crack in the ceiling. I looked up and did indeed see some small clouds appearing through the cracks, but quickly worked out and announced to the whole class that they must be dust particles as the roof space was probably not only full of dust, but also temporarily open to the elements due to some fascia wood having been removed for repair or replacement. The class seemed quite impressed with my building knowledge, so I put in another couple of token sniff checks before returning to my chair. I was also beginning to wonder if a conspiracy was afoot to derail the test. This had started to happen in a previous geography lesson that week until I announced that as the test had to be completed that week and no other time was available, the class would have to sit it again during one of their lunch hours. Subsequently, the sickness and stomach aches that many of the class had been experiencing miraculously disappeared!

Much to my annoyance most of the class now seemed to be fidgeting and looking up to the ceiling. Another boy said that he could also smell smoke, but I was more interested in the fact that he had not put his hand up and, furthermore, the quiet of the test was being disrupted. I reprimanded and warned him and despite a few 'buts' he quietened down. But peace was far from restored. I was convinced that I was right (one of my worst faults) and was becoming more and more immune towards any dissenting voice from the 'dust' theory, but I was still faced with a class not doing their test properly so decided to quash the rival smoke theory once and for all. I noticed an inspection hatch in the ceiling roughly in the centre of the room and announced that the test was going to be stopped for a few minutes and that if we lost any more time after I had checked the loft, we would have to continue into the lunch period. I felt confident that none of the class would want to miss food or football.

I asked the boy at the desk immediately below the hatch to move and after checking that his desk was not likely to collapse, began to climb onto the desk via a chair. As I was doing this, one of the less well-behaved members of 1B suggested quite loudly that letting in some air would be dangerous if there was a fire, but by now I was so convinced of a conspiracy theory that I didn't even notice the increased amount of smoke emanating from not only the edges of the hatch, but also a series of cracks around the ceiling. I pushed the hatch firmly but it didn't move. Another boy shouted 'No, sir!' as I gave it a much bigger thump, but he was too late. The hatch swung open on a hinge and I thrust my head up into the roof space. At that moment a flame seemed to surge towards me from a beam about ten feet away, which encouraged me to duck quickly, but not quickly enough! My face had been saved from plastic surgery but the hair had been singed to such an extent that my conversion from New Romantic to Punk Rocker was almost instantaneous.

I learnt subsequently that one of the builders had been using a blow torch to remove some flaking paint from just under the gutter outside our classroom and that unknown to him he had set light to a crack in the wood before going to his lunch break. The wind must have fanned this small flame inwards before I added fuel to the fire, literally, by supplying it with the required oxygen rush at precisely the right moment to 'boost' its power and set fire to some very old and dry roof beams.

I was in shock for a few seconds, which allowed the air to fuel the flames even more, so that when I did eventually close the hatch a roaring fire could now be heard in the roof space and I had a slightly burnt hand.

I jumped off the table and before words could come out, pointed towards the fire bell. A gleeful pupil took his cue for permitted damage and grabbed my board rubber, successfully breaking the glass on his second attempt.

By now I had recovered myself and told the pupils to stand up, leave everything on their desks and make their way to the fire exit which was a metal staircase on one side of this top-floor classroom.

For some reason a boy rushed to the exit, held his hand up as if to stop anything coming near him and shouted, 'No! Sir, we can't.' I interrupted him at this point as we needed to move quickly with lives at risk but he stayed put and uttered, 'But Sir, we can't go that way, it's closed while the builders are here!' He was right of course; in fact the bottom half of the stairway had been dismantled for urgent repair, a fact I should have remembered. A brief vision of boys cascading off the staircase lemming-like flashed before me before I acknowledged this information with a quick, 'Well done Billy,' before asking the lads to leave by the normal door. 'No running!'

As I shepherded my class through the school a number of teachers asked me what was going on as they had obviously worked out that I was nearest to the problem (and had a singed head) and I gave them a brief account omitting my 'stupid' moments.

By the time I had my class lined up on the field and had completed a head count, a few flames were coming out of the side of the roof. Had I destroyed the building? Was my teaching career at an end? Was the building insured?

I looked round the field. No one in particular was looking at me, thankfully, but the boys were far more agitated than usual with all the excitement. Even one or two of the really 'hard' teachers were having a little bit of trouble getting their forms quiet.

The headmaster arrived on the scene, glared at the pupils, and an uneasy quiet descended. He asked if everyone was out of the school and the secretary with responsibility for registers confirmed that this was the case. I breathed a sigh of relief. At least I wasn't a murderer! He then asked the caretaker to open the school gates to allow the fire brigade in and so off he dashed to collect his bunch of master keys. A minute or so later he reappeared and sprinted with commendable speed to the gates where after a few moments fumbling he attempted to unlock the padlock. I wondered why it was taking so long and had to fend off one or two difficult questions about my hair from two pupils and a teacher, when suddenly he looked at the bunch for a few seconds before rushing back to the head exclaiming, 'I'm sorry Sir, it's the wrong keys.' This news resulted in a spontaneous cheer from the lads, obviously hoping for a few weeks, or even longer, off school if the damage was substantial, but as the head swung round towards them only sniggering faces remained. A teacher commented quite loudly that flames could be seen coming out from some tiles and the response this time was a loud 'Burn! ... Burn!' which was again largely quelled by the head.

Loud sirens could now be heard outside and a few seconds later two fire engines rushed onto the scene. This sparked a very loud 'Boo!' from the boys followed by a few chants of 'Let it burn!' from somewhere near the back of the lines.

By now the head had been reunited with his favourite megaphone and issued a final warning which at least stopped any more chanting, but the atmosphere was still far from settled.

The firemen had located the nearest water connection point and after an impressive and speedy display had unrolled the hoses and began to douse the flames. A much larger flame leapt up momentarily before I saw with relief that some missing fascias were allowing the water to penetrate the roof space and within about ten minutes the flames seem to have gone out and the amount of smoke had also reduced.

Within fifteen minutes it was even possible for a fireman to inspect the roofspace from a ladder and another to check the loft from the hatch in the classroom.

I can't describe my relief when I heard the leader of the team report to the head that the fire was out and that we were very lucky as even a few more minutes would have resulted in a seriously spreading fire. As it was only a few roof timbers were charred with no real structural damage. There was a final cheer, however, from the boys when the head announced that lunch would be extended for one hour as the firemen needed to be sure that the fire was completely out. He also pointed out that the endangered wing of the school would be out of bounds until further notice, which prompted some animated conversation amongst those boys who were going to 'escape' certain lessons that afternoon and have a 'break' on the field instead.

The staff were asked to gather round the head and with commendable team spirit, we had quickly arranged a rota of volunteers to supervise the pupils during the extended lunch break.

I had half an hour off and was keen to hide away somewhere to gather my thoughts and think up a suitable story that wasn't too much of a lie and also didn't make me look too stupid. I noticed the head look at me in rather a strange way (perhaps he had seen my giveaway new hair style?) and fully expected him to order me to stop, but I made it to the P.E. teachers' staffroom which was thankfully empty. There then followed a few minutes of deliberation, combined with mild panic. How could I explain my actions at the inevitable interrogation that was to follow?

I was still considering my options when a knock came on the door. It was a prefect holding a piece of paper that I recognised immediately. It was the head's light blue-coloured tear-off note pad.

'Please come to my office when you are not on playground duty,' were the stark words that greeted me and as I still had at least twenty minutes of 'free' time left I had no option but to face the music.

The head had a wonderful talent for using seemingly friendly and innocuous introductions as a means of relaxing the interviewee before striking a telling blow with a carefully-worded phrase designed to get to 'the truth', and so when I was greeted with, 'Well, quite a morning Peter, I thought the drill went pretty well, didn't you?' I knew that my death sentence was about to follow.

With reference to my new hairstyle he then commented, 'Are you OK? You seem to have burnt your hair and hand ... how did that happen?'

I decided that under the steely gaze of the head my only option was the truth with a slight adjustment. I proceeded to tell him the whole story omitting some of the pupils' assistance and also creating the impression that the fire was already 'roaring' before I was forced to open the hatch to confirm the need for a rapid evacuation. There were a few tremors in my voice as I delivered this account, but as no one was dead or in hospital the head seemed content to accept this version of events. He did finish, however, with a suggestion that opening a hatch to a potential fire could make it flare up, although in this case 'it was obviously already burning quite a lot!' I left with more than a suspicion that he knew the truth but was prepared to bask in the positives, particularly the fact that the fire drill had gone so well in a real situation. 'It's good that the lads realise how serious a real fire could be! Bye Peter,' was his final remark.

My relief at having escaped fairly lightly was tempered over the next few days by the usual Smart Alecs on the staff who must have either worked out what had happened, or possibly had received the full story from one of the class I had been teaching.(I did consider issuing some sort of veiled threat to the class about talking about my role in the affair, but decided against it as I would really be in trouble if found guilty of trying to bully the little lovelies into changing a story for my benefit.)

The morning after the fire found me inching my way up to the staff notice board in the hope that I had not been given a dreaded cover!

As an aside, it was quite interesting to observe teachers' reactions to the cover list. To many it was merely a shrug of the shoulders as they acknowledged the inevitable, whereas others would immediately about-turn out of the staffroom at pace. In some cases it turned out to be the ruination of not only the teacher's day, but also the poor pupils who had them for the first lesson or two, especially if the teacher concerned had received a lot of recent covers and was covering for the same teacher yet again!

I had, however, escaped on this occasion and with a satisfied sigh was turning towards my favourite seat when I noticed my name at the top of a list of volunteers for a five-week health and safety course. A quick glance around the staffroom at the usual suspects did not reveal who the guilty person was, although one or two of the 'lads' seemed to be deliberately avoiding my gaze. As I rubbed my name off there were some rather loud coughs but again I couldn't be sure where they came from.

As I sat down, John began to chat with me and suggested in response to the head's request to broaden the nature of the annual inter-house competitions (The Cock House Cup) we could have a cooking competition, which could be called 'The Coq au Vin Cup'. I suggested (in jest of course) that he mentioned this idea at the next staff meeting, but he declined pointing out that there were other more 'burning' issues to be dealt with.

By the following week I seemed to have escaped any further mention of the fire and on a lovely sunny morning, found myself being driven to early morning golf by Steve who, noticing I seemed a little sleepy, suggested he should play one of his new disco albums. As 'Burn baby burn, disco inferno' belted out from his impressive car speakers I had no option but to give in to a full belly laugh!

Once a boy always a boy

Why is it that male P.E. teachers never seem to grow up and yet the females are nearly always extremely sensible? Perhaps men choose the profession because they want to continue to be able to 'play' as they get older, or is it just in the hormones? Put a few guys together and throw in some beer, plus perhaps a competitive situation, or the need to impress accompanying women and it can often result in some unusual, even childish, behaviour.

I must quickly add that I am not referring to the everyday work of the male of the P.E. species. I have been lucky to have worked almost entirely with teachers of both sexes whose work in school with colleagues and pupils alike has been exemplary ... no, it is the 'off duty' moments where strange things happen!

I'll take an outdoor pursuit weekend I attended many years ago with some colleagues as an example. This was set up by a school wishing to promote their outdoor centre in Wales and encourage other local schools to take groups to the venue in the Black Mountains. So, about thirty P.E. teachers set off in various ways on the road west.

The 'fun' started almost immediately as about six of us were told to cram into the back of a rather rickety van without seats for the journey (this was many years before health and safety was 'god'). We later found out that the two spare front seats were occupied not, as we had been told, by essential provisions, but by a rather large ghetto blaster (I told you it was an old story) and a variety of food supplies for our intrepid driver. The explanation for this was that he had not wanted to show any favouritism to anyone, said with a glint in his eye.

The trip in the back was becoming very uncomfortable for everyone, so I suggested we passed the time with a game of charades, which resulted in a combination of groans and silence from the rest. My second idea was to introduce ourselves, which would also serve to break the ice for the rest of the weekend. This was met with slightly fewer groans, but a rather large rugby player sprawled in the corner murmured 'I just want to sleep' which seemed to end the subject.

About ten minutes later, however, I was surprised to hear another gentleman suggest that it might pass the time and that if I started with introducing myself, then anyone who wanted to follow suit could do so. This seemed to meet with general approval, including 'Mr Grumpy' who uttered a semi-desperate 'Whatever!' which was I suppose a sort of agreement to continue (and also a phrase twenty years ahead of its time). I managed to curtail the epic nature of my life and interests to about five minutes and sure enough everyone subsequently contributed at least a minute or two, resulting in a series of conversations that helped to pass the next hour or so.

Meanwhile, in one of the other cars, things were much more exciting as the driver and his accomplice executed their first practical joke of the weekend.

Two teachers from the same school were involved in the plot and the victim was another passenger. On approaching the Severn Bridge the driver asked the victim to hand over his passport to the co-driver to speed up the border crossing into Wales. He was, however, a little puzzled and stated that he thought that Wales was part of the UK and that passports were not required. He half suspected a wind-up, but the fact that the others had brought their passports was one factor which made him question his own understanding of the situation, and, when the driver pulled over and explained to him with a very straight and concerned face, that membership of the EU and the recent spate of IRA attacks on the mainland had altered the regulations, he started to become quite worried.

The driver apologised for not including 'bring your passport' on the information sheet for the weekend, as he assumed he had known the rules. By now the victim's weekend looked like it was going to end before it had even started, with a miserable train journey back to London and away from all the fun, so he made a desperate plea to the others for a way out of the situation. Could they not just talk to someone at the border crossing and hand over some other ID? The plotters had prepared for this request and the co-driver proceeded to explain how the same thing had happened last year when an individual was refused entry into Wales.

After a few minutes of pretend-thinking the driver came up with a plan, which was to hide the victim in the boot until they had crossed the border. 'You'll have to be very quiet until we let you out. There's also often some police patrols just over the border, so it may be a little while.'

I can't remember if he actually ended up in the boot, but if so I expect that he stayed there for a long time!

Back in our van the journey had continued relatively smoothly, apart from an incident at a motorway service station when the driver decided to leave one of the ladies in the loo, drive off about one hundred yards and hide behind a large lorry. Her initial surprise at the disappearance of the van soon deteriorated into mild panic until about five minutes later, we convinced the driver that the joke had gone far enough and we returned to pick up a very angry young lady.

I found out later on that the driver was getting a little fed up with her constant talking, which he said was partly my fault for instigating the 'life story' idea. Unfortunately for him, her anger at such an 'unbeliev-ably childish joke' meant that she did not stop talking about it and remonstrating with the driver until we reached our destination.

The rather basic bunk beds in the 'boys' dormitory seemed to be very comfortable compared with the discomfort of the van and the first night went relatively peacefully, except for a rubber snake in the bottom of one lady's sleeping bag which drew a very impressive scream, and a fake fire alarm which got everyone out of bed at 2a.m. As well as being very childish, a number of us actually thought this was irresponsible as we would now question the validity of any future alarm, but to be fair to 'the pranksters' they did explain that this was not the correct sound and proceeded to play the real fire alarm.

The first morning dawned murky and very wet, so the proposed rock climbing session was postponed and replaced with an introductory canoe session in the local sports centre pool.

The highlight of this was the last thirty minutes when everyone was going to have a go at an Eskimo roll. I had always wanted to learn this skill, probably as a result of a number of uncomfortable exits from upside-down canoes in the river Medway in Kent. The reality of the cold and shock felt nothing like the relatively graceful and warm practice sessions we had had in a swimming pool! I remember in particular my first real capsize (in the Medway) when I had tried to exit so rapidly that I almost became jammed into the cockpit. This resulted in a lot of gasping and flapping to extricate myself, not to mention the grazed knees. Oblivious to any shouted instructions I then struck out for the bank and scrambled up a few feet, only to dive back into the water almost immediately as the bank was completely covered in stinging nettles. The instructor's comment 'Oh Peter, that wasn't a good example for the kids,' didn't help matters as my head and hands pulsated from the multiple stings. I subsequently learnt that to just wait a few seconds in the upside-down position before doing anything, to gather your thoughts, is the best way forward.

It was, however, in a fairly confident state of mind that I awaited my turn at the Eskimo roll as I had at least become quite used to being upside-down and the pool was lovely and warm. It was also amusing to watch some of the failed attempts, particularly the super-strong rugby player (Mr Grumpy again), who was so convinced that all that was required was brute strength that he never actually got close to completing the manoeuvre. His humiliation was complete when our instructor told him to get out of the water and watch a rather small lady complete the roll three times in succession with a combination of good technique and a minimum of effort. He didn't try again!

And so my turn arrived. Bob and Jim, two teachers I knew well were positioned at either end of the canoe for safety and advice and as I had seen them both complete the roll earlier, this was an extra bonus. The instructor gave me some final reminders, in particular to try and use the momentum of the initial roll to continue back to upright with a smooth and correct paddle action under water.

My first attempt was not too bad and as my head appeared above the water line I was able to grab a breath and try again. However after a couple more failed attempts I was in need of some air and a rest, so I banged the bottom of the canoe as a pre-arranged signal that I was going to exit under water, which I executed smoothly and calmly.

Bob and Jim were very encouraging and told me that I had almost succeeded on the first and third attempts. They ushered away the instructor convincing him that I was doing fine and off we went again. Jim suggested that if I didn't quite complete the roll I should pause for a second in the upside-down position before concentrating fully on power and technique.

As I rose from another unsuccessful four or five attempts I was becoming a little weary and angry with myself for not completing a manoeuvre I thought was well within my capabilities. But Bob and Jim were adamant that I was on the verge of success.

I looked around and saw at least three of my colleagues complete the roll with ease and style. One even managed three in a row and as she shouted exultantly, 'Wow! And I've never even been in a canoe before!' my determination to succeed became even more intense. In addition, a number of the group were now gathered round the edge of the pool watching my efforts with barely-concealed smiles.

As one of the ladies shouted 'Go on Pete, you can do it!' I told Bob and Jim that I was going to 'give it everything' this time. This drew a round of applause and more encouragement from the side. I was ready!

I gathered myself for one last attempt and once again tipped the canoe sideways. With a mighty underwater 'swoosh' I surfaced, but just as I thought I had succeeded I slipped back under. Another massive sweep brought me even closer to success, a fact confirmed by cries of 'Oh nearly!' from the poolside which I heard before descending once more into the deep.

My next few attempts were getting ever more ragged and eventually I was not only unable to take in any breaths but had also drunk a considerable amount of chlorinated water.

Eventually I was reduced to a pathetic, flapping water beast who had not only lost technique, but also, almost the will to live. I hung upside-down one last time before admitting defeat and slithering out and back to the surface where I received some sympathetic applause but also a smattering of laughter. My humiliation was complete when the lady who had completed the multiple rolls told me that with one or two adjustments to my technique she was sure I would complete the manoeuvre next time. This would have been bad enough by itself, but she then joined a group of about six or seven others who, after she said a few words, could hardly hide their amusement at my failings.

It was only later that evening that Nigel, a colleague from my school told me the truth. Bob and Jim had briefed everyone beforehand about what was going to happen. Being positioned at either end of the canoe they were perfectly placed to not only keep encouraging me, but also by holding on to the end of the canoe, tip me back under at just the moment I thought I had achieved 'glory'. The poolside spectators were also told to keep encouraging me and the combination of all these factors, added to my own pride, made me persevere for much longer than was reasonable. They had also decided to not quite drown me, which was nice of them!

Despite choking up a good deal of lunch which obviously did not mix well with chlorine, I did see the funny side of things and my pride was restored a year later when I managed a roll on a hot day on the dreaded river Medway, when I was so warm I was just dying to cool off!

The weather had become dry by the afternoon with even the occasional glimpse of sun, so the rock climbing was back on. A short drive through the Black Mountains (same van, but a shorter period of pain) brought us to a disused rock quarry and the prospect of some easy to moderately difficult climbs. I had some climbing experience thanks to a series of outdoor pursuit week-ends over the years, but would describe myself as no more than competent. It was, however, an early chance to redeem myself after 'the drowning' and I made a mental note not to attempt anything out of my comfort zone to be sure of success.

The resident rock-climbing expert had been drafted in from another South London school and we settled down as he reminded us of the various safety issues. It was about five minutes into his brief when I noticed a few small stones and other debris falling onto the ground behind him. I thought of suggesting that he moved further away from the edge, but the debris seemed to have stopped falling after a few minutes. As he was nearing the end of his talk, however, some more and slightly larger stones fell behind him. I pointed this out to him and he quickly moved forward, at the same time turning round and looking up (as we all did) to see Jim merrily climbing the quarry face without any safety rope, dislodging some of the rock face as he went.

Pretending to ignore this act of stupidity, our instructor finished off his safety briefing and then divided us into groups according to experience and ability. I placed myself into the 'some experience of climbing' team, which numbered about seven. At this moment Jim shouted down, 'Is it time for the safety briefing yet?' which the instructor completely ignored!

By the time we were roped up and ready to go he had descended by the same route and was busily trying to apologise to the instructor who was intent on placing him in the 'bottom' group as punishment for his 'dangerous and unprofessional behaviour'. After much pleading and grovelling he was promoted to a better group, but still one below his obvious natural ability.

The afternoon was very satisfactory from my point of view as I not only managed to complete all the set climbs, but also ascended with a gazelle-like smoothness and grace that probably reflected the relative ease of the climbs rather than any good ability on my behalf.

The icing on the cake was that I was, in addition, able to assist some less experienced climbers with some useful tips with regard to both climbing and the handling of the safety rope. The final moment of sweetness was when the instructor complemented me on an observation I had made to one of the Eskimo roll superstars about a slight improvement she could make with her hand position on the safety rope. Life was back on an even keel and my canoe failings a distant memory.

It was in this fairly smug state that I settled down against a rock to enjoy a well-earned snack bar and cup of warm coffee, although the afternoon was by now so pleasant that we were in shirt sleeves.

I had almost nodded off when the murmur of ladies' voices began to stir me. At first I just had a blurry vision of some arms pointing towards a white object on the quarry wall, but as I became more alert I realised that about four of the ladies on the trip had become concerned about a sheep that seemed to be rather precariously perched on a ledge about thirty feet up. Actually, it was happily munching away at a tasty growth of much greener grass than was probably available in and around the rather 'bare' quarry. Nevertheless, they were concerned and at least three of them gasped 'Oh!' as the sheep slipped slightly. Mr Grumpy (rugby) came over and made the sensible observation that if the sheep had managed to get down, there would be even less difficulty in going back up. He also commented that he had often seen sheep in similar seemingly precarious positions and was yet to see one fall. The girls were not convinced by this speech, however, possibly influenced by the general feeling amongst the group that he was somewhat arrogant.

This was my chance to turn redemption into glory! St George to slay the dragon and save the sheep! It only took me a few moments to decide that the height from the ground was not life threatening and that there seemed to be a fairly clear scrambling route up to the poor beast. If my mind needed making up any more, it was when one of the girls looked at me, before uttering an 'Oh dear' and pointing up the slope. I went over to the ladies to discuss the matter and sure enough their collective love of animals plus the desire not to witness a dead sheep at their feet meant that a few minutes later I had been transformed into 'Sheep Rescue Man'. What on earth I was going to do if I even managed to reach the beast had not even entered my mind!

Intent on no slip-ups, I began to climb after bravely ignoring concerns about my safety from one or two of the girls. I had also chosen my moment to start the ascent as that when the instructor had driven off to take some equipment back to the lodge. I didn't want to be accused of 'doing a Jim'!

My first few steps using hands and feet were reasonably smooth, but I was a little concerned about the unstable nature of the rock face at this point. Within a few seconds a lump of grass that had looked like a good hand-hold had come away in my hand and I decided to re-assess my actions. Looking down I noticed that the drop was probably less than I had originally calculated and also that if I did slip it would result in an uncomfortable slide to the bottom with at worst a few cuts and bruises rather than any broken bones. I looked up to the sheep who was still happily munching away, oblivious to the human drama unfolding below.

I inched my way upwards and soon found myself quite close to my target. The sheep looked round somewhat startled and quickly rushed forwards a few feet onto a slightly more precarious ledge. I looked down. Two of the girls had their hands covering their eyes. Was the sheep's wellbeing still upmost in their thoughts or were they just worried about me? At this point I realised I hadn't really thought out how I was going to save the sheep and this caused me some acute embarrassment for a few moments until I saw a much wider ledge gradually leading to the ground just in front of the sheep. If I could nudge him or her that way I would achieve my mission! I edged forward again, but this time the sheep didn't move. Again I moved sideways until I was so close to the sheep's rear that I could hear munching from the other end. As I made my next move, which was intended to be a gentle slap on the back to encourage a few steps towards the safe path, the sheep suddenly swung round so quickly that his head whacked into my nose with some force. For a moment victim and saviour were face to face and I couldn't help thinking that the 'Baa' from the sheep and his or her curious expression could probably be translated into 'What are you doing up here, idiot?'

I checked my nose, which was bruised, but not bloodied. This sudden arm movement may have been interpreted as some kind of threat and the startled beast swung back round, but instead of taking the safe route back to earth, leaped up and sideways a good few feet onto what looked like a particularly precarious, narrow ledge.

I looked down at the gathering crowd of spectators and noticed even more hands covering faces and a few others shaking their heads sideways. I looked up and realised that to follow the sheep any further could have meant disaster for us both! I was already approaching safety rope territory and I also finally realised that the sheep would have a greater chance of survival if I left it alone.

So I began an embarrassing descent, which involved much slipping and sliding and ended in a particularly long final slide, which left me covered in a lot of greeny-brown slime. As I moved away from the rock face I also semi-crumpled as a result of slightly twisting my ankle on landing.

My apologies to the girls were met with a few comments regarding the sheep's even more perilous position and one or two suggestions that 'It would have been better off left alone!' which I couldn't disagree with.

At that moment the instructor drove back in to the quarry and to my surprise no one 'ratted' on me, for which I was very grateful.

When we left, a number of the group looked up at the sheep with a further shake of the head before we scrambled into the bus and one of the men even tried to make me feel better by saying that he was sure that left by itself the sheep would find a safe route up or down. Mercifully, the instructor had been too preoccupied with packing up and making announcements to notice a sheep in peril.

Bob suggested a sing-song on the way back and volunteered to start, giving a fine rendition of 'Baa Baa Black Sheep' and sure enough everyone except me and one or two who felt sorry for me, joined in. This was accompanied by much giggling and for the remainder of the short trip I was also treated to the occasional very sad 'bleat'.

I was a troubled man, which was a combination of my own stupid actions, going against so many safety issues that I had been taught and believed in, as well as a genuine concern for the sheep's life.

I found it hard to sleep that night, although one of my roommates did suggest that it may help if I counted sheep. Another told me not to worry. 'If the sheep's fallen you'll never know about it anyway!'

Little did I know that on the final morning after some more banter and 'sheep concern' at breakfast, our route to the final day's activity, potholing, had been deliberately rearranged by 'The Three Pranksteteers', Bob, Jim and Paul, to pass by the dreaded quarry!

Bob and Jim were in my van and also cranked up the pressure by constantly mentioning that they hoped the sheep had survived the night.

Then Bob told me that we were approaching the quarry. My heartbeat raised a few beats as the van cleared a corner and the rock face came into view. My heart leapt as a quick scan of the face showed that it was sheepless, but then sank as one of the ladies started to moan as she pointed out a large white fluffy bundle on the ground, on its back with four legs pointing skyward and motionless!

I felt as if the earth could swallow me up and this was compounded even further as another two ladies began to sob and one shouted that I should have 'left it alone!' The final insult was when Bob rather cruelly offered to get me a T-shirt printed with 'sheep slayer' printed on the front in large red letters!

A mile or so further on the van came abruptly to a halt. Jim (driving) took a deep sigh and then turned to me saying, 'Fos, I know this is tough, but we have to bury that sheep! There may be some other climbers going to the area today and as it is quite warm it could really smell bad soon and also attract a lot of flies! I brought a couple of shovels just in case.' He brought two shovels out of a sack and waved them in front of me.

How much worse could this day get? But as everyone in the van quickly agreed to Jim's suggestion, it was a few minutes later that I had got out of the van at the crime scene. Bob had suggested that as I was the 'killer' I should first go and make sure the sheep was dead. I walked up to the carcass, not sure if I really wanted to find a severely crippled sheep rather than a dead one! As I got closer I could see no leg movement, but also surprisingly no splattered blood. Within about ten feet I realised that the lack of leg movement was not attributable to death, but the fact that the legs were very well crafted sticks complete with stone hoofs. The body was also a masterpiece consisting of a sack full of earth surrounded with genuine wool carefully gathered from the surrounding area, including an abundance present on barbed wire where the sheep often scraped and rubbed their backs etc.

The only unconvincing part of the sculpture was the head, which was initially hidden from my view as I had approached from the sheep's tail end.

I had been done again!!! At precisely the moment I turned round to the van, everyone started to joyfully sing 'Baa Baa Black Sheep'!

My relief at the fact that the sheep was probably still alive was, however, a stronger feeling than any embarrassment I may have felt and I joined in and enjoyed the general banter about sheep. I also reminded myself that practically everyone had been the victim of some sort of prank that weekend with one 'innocent' being at the top of the list with an unassailable six events, including itching powder in his sleeping bag, a suspicious wet patch on his bed (a mixture of orange juice and milk) and a deliberately rigged orienteering course (optional night activity) twice as long as anyone else's. He arrived at the pub just as it was closing!

I had mixed emotions about potholing (and was also not looking forward to the long and uncomfortable drive back to Bromley that evening). As we kitted up for our descent into the depths of the Black Mountains my thoughts drifted back to an outdoor pursuits trip a few years earlier when I had found the narrow spaces and darkness a far from enjoyable experience, especially when it was required to contort the body first down and then up a narrow, slippery U-bend in the rock structure. A colleague on the same trip had had an even worse experience, however. He was a well-built rugby player who found himself faced with a rather small hole he had to squeeze through. The students' smaller frames slipped through easily and even I managed to get through reasonably comfortably once I had eased my broad shoulders through with a little bit of wiggling and sideways lean. Grant, however, had less room for manoeuvre and found himself stuck halfway. The more he tried to struggle the more jammed in he seemed to become. Eventually he was not only completely stuck, but also convinced that the rocks around him were moving and starting to crush his chest. To anyone watching, this was of course impossible as the rock face was completely solid and strong, but he was becoming irrational and beginning to panic. Our guide tried to calm him by explaining that he was in fact increasing his chest size due to rapid breathing and anxiety, but even after five minutes of concentrated calming exercises he was stuck fast. In the end our instructor had to go round to his 'head end' and manoeuvre his arms and shoulders into such a position that he could come out the way he had gone in. He was close to fainting and vowed never to go potholing again!

There was one manoeuvre that I wasn't looking forward to. This involved having to swim through flooded sections far underground. I was keeping my fingers crossed that we did not have to negotiate such an obstacle. My concern was aggravated by the fact that we had been issued with wet suits. I daren't ask why! Still, I had managed to complete the course a few years earlier and didn't seem to suffer from claustrophobia. There was also the promise of visiting one or two large caverns, complete with small rivers, which sounded quite exciting!

And so we set of into the darkness. I was with two of 'The Pranksters', Bob and Paul, but they seemed strangely muted during the first half an hour or so, so perhaps they were slightly anxious about being underground as well.

We came into a rather large cave and our guide pointed out some interesting rock features before indicating our direction with his torch. Bob, however, asked him to wait a moment and then enquired how long it was before we arrived at a cave with some lighting and stalactites. He also asked when we were going to get into a rowing boat and float through some larger caves with Pan pipes in the background.

The instructor took this wind-up at face value and proceeded to defend the natural beauty of the caves. Bob pretended to be extremely disappointed, even going so far as to suggest that he had been dragged underground under false pretences and wanted to go back. The instructor's slightly sharp reply was that it was probably easier to continue in the same direction and so off we went as Bob sneaked me a smile and wink. I reminded him that we should be treating the instructor with a lot more respect as without him we would be lost. I emphasised this point by momentarily turning off both our lights to enhance the danger of our situation should we be left alone with dead batteries! He apologised to the instructor explaining that 'it was only meant as a joke', but as we set off again he held my arm and whispered that he was actually very afraid of being underground and had just been trying to lighten his mood with a joke or two.

I had my doubts about his honesty but said no more as I couldn't be sure. Our group was being led by the guide, with Paul in second place, myself in third and then Bob bringing up the rear. He had been third up to this point but asked for a change as he felt 'more secure' with me in front of him. Perhaps, I thought, he was worried about being directly behind a fellow prankster! Within a few minutes we arrived at the most difficult section of our subterranean journey. It was one of the dreaded U-bends that not only went down and then up, but also had some water at the bottom. It also seemed to be an extremely small opening!

I asked our guide if the passage was completely submerged and to my relief he said that it wasn't and that the water was just a puddle, which had collected at the bottom of the bend. 'That's why we are all wearing wetsuits, plus they are better than normal clothes for sliding along wet rocks.' He then told us to relax as we slid through, to stay in a stretched position and to create a bit of forward momentum as we slid down. We were then to arch our backs upwards as we reached the bottom with hopefully enough momentum to carry us up the other side. He would help to pull anyone who needed help through by going first. We were to wait for his shout before setting off one at a time. He then proceeded to almost dive headfirst down the slippery slope and then disappear gracefully with hardly a movement of his legs. A few seconds later he called for Paul to head off into the unknown. His 'dive' was not so graceful and was followed by a loud thud as he had lifted his head too far. Being now a little stuck he tried to scramble his way up but had forgotten that the space he was passing through was only just high enough for a streamlined body to pass through. There followed much swearing and bashing of his safety helmet until he was heaved unceremoniously through by our resident expert. This was not at all encouraging for either Bob or me and Bob quietly pleaded with me to refuse to go on. I also had my doubts but felt that as I couldn't drown, I would survive the ordeal somehow. I had never seen Bob so close to tears as he pronounced 'Fos, I can't do this, help me please!' I looked at his lamplit face for telltale smiles etc. but could not see any clues. I pointed out to him that this was not the best place for wind-ups and that we had to go on, reminding him that as I was much larger than him he should have no problem getting through. He was not convinced and attempted to hold me back. If this was an act it was approaching Oscar-winning quality. I reminded him that it was not a sub-merged passage and then fibbed that I had actually seen the guide's hands on our side helping Paul through. He let me go and I reassured him that if he wasn't acting we would help him. By now he had his hands over his head and was bobbing up and down slowly in a crouched position (similar to Basil Fawlty under stress) repeating 'Don't leave me!' in a sort of desperate whisper.

I decided to go and report the situation to the other side who were beginning to get a little jumpy at the time we were taking. Bob would probably come if he was left alone and if not I felt sure that our guide would be better equipped to come back and coax him through. I composed myself and resolved to abandon my usual caution and go for a speedy, smooth gliding movement, which would not only impress the instructor but also show Bob that the way through was not so difficult.

I looked down into the gloom and was not reassured by the darkness and small size of the target. But with a final glance and thumbs-up to the whimpering Bob I set off with a surprisingly elegant slide. Within a second or two I was staring at the other two with my back in a beautiful arch and with hardly any bumps to show for the journey. I was told to stretch my arms forwards and to stay 'long' which I did...

My fingertips had barely touched human flesh, however, before I was quickly jerked back down about three feet, bumping my chin a few times in the process.

Bob had his hands around my ankles! I could hear him sobbing 'Pull me through, please, I can't let go!' My back was in a flexed position I was not used to and I couldn't move forwards. I thought about kicking myself free for a second or two but decided there was firstly not enough room and secondly I didn't want to injure Bob in any way. I told him to let go as I couldn't move but he was by now an incoherent wreck, so I waited for another suggestion. Our instructor tried everything from sympathy to bullying to release me but to no avail. He decided eventually to pull me through sufficiently so that he could see Bob's hands. If he then touched them, Bob would feel sufficiently reassured to release me. And so a painful (for my back, arms and legs) tug of war followed with the reluctant Bob resisting any forward motion. I now had some idea of what it must have been like to be tortured on the rack! Eventually the strength of two gradually overcame one and I was moving painfully upwards. As my ankles and Bob's hands appeared, the instructor reached down to grab his wrists and ordered him to let go of my legs. As he did so his grip slipped momentarily and Bob, complete with one of my shoes, slid out of sight. I was hauled up and there then followed some desperate shouting and scrambling from Bob until his 'pleading' arms reappeared. He was hauled unceremoniously up and proceeded to hug me and issue a stream of apologies, plus a further plea to get out as soon as possible.

I asked him where my shoe was and he pointed apologetically back into the hole. The instructor was quite angry by now and told him to go back and get it. Bob begged him not to send him back and after a few minutes of wasted negotiation, it fell to the instructor to retrieve the completely sodden shoe. It was cold and uncomfortable to wear, but preferable to cutting my feet on a rock, so I struggled on for the remaining half hour or so of our ordeal.

We eventually reappeared on the surface and Bob took me aside to plead with me not to tell anyone else about his behaviour as he didn't want to 'lose face' with his peers. I said that I would think about it, pleased that I had a sort of blackmail situation that I was sure would save me from any further pranks.

We rejoined the rest of the potholers who had had a mixture of experiences underground, including one 'refuser' who had to be escorted back to the start. I looked over to Bob who placed his hands momentarily in a praying position as he looked pleadingly towards me ...Yes, I had him ... at least so I thought until Jim shouted over to us, 'How did it go lads? Did you keep up with "The Mole", Bob? And did anyone beat his record of five seconds on the U-bend?' I looked over to Bob who was giving me a big smile and a double thumbs-up!

And so ended an eventful weekend, apart from one or two minor stings from a now satisfied team of pranksters

147

on the way home. For all the years I knew them it was not easy to work out if Jim, Bob and Paul were being serious or not and yet they were all excellent teachers and a picture of good behaviour in front of a class.

Let's end with a prankster from another school.

He had for a number of years organised a golf and tennis trip to south west France with a combination of pupils and staff who enjoyed these sports. It was, however, the first trip for one of the teachers and he was so impressed with the activities, facilities and accommodation that he was seriously considering taking his own family there in the future.

On the coach trip home he was approached by John who, hearing of his interest, kindly presented him with a promotional video about the resort to show his wife, for which he was a little surprised, but very grateful.

A few days later his wife studied the very impressive picture of the resort on the video cover and suggested that the whole family (including kids of about four and eight) watched it that evening. The video was put into the player and all settled down to a thirty-minute preview of their next holiday ... unfortunately the label had been switched from a Swedish pornographic film involving naked nurses, a sauna and a selection of so called 'friends'. It took about twenty seconds of wide-eyed staring before the video was stopped and a further minute before John received a phone call announcing a complete break in their friendship etc. which was later commuted to a three-week stand off after John explained that he had said the video was for 'you and the wife!'

School Dinners

Yummy! Yummy! Yummy! One more will do... Yummy! That's what I think about school dinners.

There was nothing better to look forward to after a cold winter's morning out on the school field than a good old fashioned school meal ... Fish and chips on Friday, chicken curry midweek, or a gorgeous lasagne to keep our European credentials up to scratch – it mattered not! I just happened to be lucky enough throughout my teaching career to be blessed with, not only good school cooks, but also individuals who understood the needs of a strapping P.E. teacher's stomach, especially the puddings! Apple crumble, Spotted dick and all the others ... lovely!

I even enjoyed the more recent moves towards 'healthier' food in school including the great pastas and salads I devoured on my reduced calorie eating periods.

But Friday was always 'treat' day. And although the healthy options were still available, there was a plethora of comfort food to warm even the coldest heart.

And yet this seems not to be the case half a century earlier, when I was at school, or is my memory just being selective?

149

I still remember some of my favourite puddings at both my primary and secondary school, but the main courses have left a different taste. In particular, the only semi-warm lamb (or was it mutton?) which appeared at least twice a week at my primary school was not a dish I relished. It also had quite a lot of fat attached to it, tasteless gravy and a selection of lukewarm and flaccid vegetables as the final accompaniment.

Although my pudding memories are better, I must also include semolina and rice pudding on 'the hate list'. In the latter case, however, I have had a recent rethink when a sweetener (i.e. honey) has been included and it is actually hot!

My teaching career was blessed, however, with the exception of my second school, a rather sad place in the centre of London, which had fallen on such bad times due to a series of very poor intakes and a failure to inject money into the fabric of the building, that it didn't have a canteen and instead, the staff and pupils were subjected to awful pre-packaged affairs that were reheated on site. I think these were the only two years in my teaching career when I 'gave up' and brought sandwiches.

The canteen at Quernmore School, Bromley, in the '70s and '80s was no more than a glorified shack and yet the ladies and gentleman of the canteen produced delights on a daily basis and even found time to make shortbread, bread pudding and other delicacies for the staff to munch on at breaktime, complete with a hot cup of coffee delivered by a duty prefect, either out on the playground or to other far flung regions of 'patrol' such as the front gates.

The cooks and their assistants all managed this with a cheerful smile and genuine caring attitude towards both staff and pupils, despite having to begin their prep at a much earlier hour than most teachers arrived at school. There was also an added, unscripted dimension to their work.

I remember clearly being approached on more than one occasion by a cook at Quernmore, about a boy whose appearance, behaviour, or loss of weight might be an indication of lack of care at home. These instances were rare, but needed to be handled with delicacy and although often the problem was nothing more than a temporary dislike of some types of food etc. or teenage angst, on occasions, despite a good lunch, there still seemed to be something wrong with an individual.

I remember one such report eventually resulting in a home visit by the local authority that revealed a home life not only consisting of practically no parental care due to a serious drug problem with both parents, but also a complete absence of money for food or heating as it was all being used to satisfy the need for drugs.

The boy eventually found a foster family and did remarkably well considering his background of severe neglect, but as the story was unfolding it was also the kitchen who helped.

The head chef was a lovely caring soul who arranged for the lad to come and do some light work in the dining hall before and after school. He was always very early to school, probably to escape the miseries of home and one cold winter's day she invited him in out of the cold to help set out the chairs and tables that were required for the first food event of the day, the breakfast club, as they were stacked to the side to cater for the various evening classes that took place in the building. (The 'club' had been recommended and funded by the local authority to fill the stomachs of pupils whose families could either not afford a breakfast for their child, or more realistically, considering the relatively cheap cost of a loaf of bread or a pack of cereals, couldn't be bothered to provide one!)

After a few days of this she asked him if he would like some free breakfast as he 'had earned it' and there was 'always some left over' and he heartily agreed to this idea, eventually volunteering (and being fed) after school as well. This of course didn't solve all of his problems, but at least provided for a basic need, which he was being denied.

I made a nostalgic visit to this school about five years after it closed as a secondary (it had been converted into a flourishing primary school, which it still is) to see some of the improvements that had been made to the building.

On walking up the drive I was relieved to notice that the main building, a very attractive mansion, hadn't been tampered with, and my pupil guide proceeded to show me round a nicely spruced up, but familiar, school. As we entered the playground area, however, there were considerable changes with pristine play areas, green trails, and one or two more permanent brick structures having replaced temporary classrooms.

My eyes then identified a huge gap on the left side of the playground where the kitchen and dining hall had once stood.

I asked about where this had gone and was subsequently led over to what was the gym in my days.

I was actually quite horrified at the prospect of food being produced and consumed here as it was already an old and poorly heated place in my time at the school. (The heating and ventilation was actually so bad that during a cold winter period, green slime would not only appear on the plastered interior, but also drip menacingly down the walls.)

I was, however, pleasantly surprised by the transformation inside. The walls were not only clean and bright but distinctly lacking in green slime. The floor was either new, or had received some remarkable remedial treatment and the damp, cold changing room had been transformed into a modern kitchen. I am not an expert in conversion and construction, but there must also have been some hidden technical advances behind this re-invigorated building.

The smells from the kitchen brought back familiar and happy memories and when the headmaster appeared and asked me if I had enjoyed my tour and would I like to stay for lunch, I could have kissed him!

A few minutes later I was easily the tallest person in the dinner queue and it was my turn to choose!

I hovered respectfully by the vegetarian option, gave the ham salad a momentary consideration, before arriving at the real decision, a Sunday roast three days before the weekend, or an equally tempting chicken curry, complete with naan bread and other relishes.

I settled on the curry as I had calculated that there would not be another at home that week and then proceeded to eye up the impressive range of desserts.

Once again, the healthy options were admirable in number, including low-fat yoghurts and fresh fruit bowls, but I was drawn like a magnet towards the rhubarb crumble. Would it be served with suitably hot and thick custard? I glanced to my left where a young man was about to be served and yes, joy of joys, a slow stream of gooey delight was inching its way from a huge ceramic jug down onto his plate. My latest healthy food intentions had been scuppered yet again and I settled down next to my guide for a delicious school meal.

To add to the enjoyment of this meal my Oliver Twist-like request for 'more' was a success and I even received some of the slightly burnt sections of crumble from the edges of the baking tray!

Fast (food) forward and I had arrived at the culinary delights of my final school (also in Bromley).

In my twenty-five years there I witnessed the changes that were occurring with regard to school meal provision.

The early eighties were to a certain extent a continuation of the good, wholesome (but not necessarily healthy) tradition, but sandwiches and salads were also beginning to appear as well as a few more continental specialities.

But it was in the nineties and the new millennium that things really changed, pushed by not only government initiatives, but also by the general public's greater awareness of health issues and a select band of celebrity chefs determined to tackle the health (and obesity) issue threatening the next generation.

As a P.E. teacher I had to support this and despite my love of hot dinners and stodgy puddings etc. I could recognise that the thinking behind these developments was sound. I was horrified to see a local news report on the television concerning a determined headteacher who had fully embraced the healthy food idea in completely revamping the menu and ingredients on offer at his school. The majority of parents had supported this move, despite moans from their children, but a small number of parents had rebelled (or perhaps they were too lazy to be firm with their children about healthier food) and had instead decided to buy fish and chips etc. and deliver this to their sons or daughters through a gap in the school playground fence at lunchtime. The film crew had captured the moment, which involved quite a bit of pushing and shoving from both parents and children, but the final 'horror' was that the parents were actually walking across the graveyard of the neighbouring church to deliver lunch. Why didn't they just provide their kids with some sandwiches for lunch and cook whatever they wanted in the evening?

Before I go off on too much of a tangent let me return to my own experiences.

As I was becoming a 'mature' member of the P.E. department it naturally coincided with me having to be more careful with my weight.

In the past all my excesses, including a love of snacking, were easily burnt off by basketball or squash training and matches, as well as simply joining in at the appropriate time during P.E. lessons.

But in my fifties my sporting week wasn't so much dedicated to further developing a six-pack and rippling muscles, but rather a battle against an ageing body! I was still pretty fit for my age, but had to start thinking about diet.

Thus from Monday to Thursday I took the healthy option more and more, but still 'let it all hang out' on Friday lunch, which was always after running club anyway!

By this time, the canteen was now reflecting not just European, but world cuisine, with a vegetarian and light, healthy option available as well.

On the other side of the playground was the new and splendid sixth-form canteen, which teaching staff were also allowed to use.

As they were often run by different catering firms, the menus were always different, although both areas had commendably embraced the healthy eating ethos.

It would be one of the highlights of my day to visit both establishments during a free moment in the morning to find out where I would be having lunch. Even now when I visit Bromley from time to time, I am occasionally allowed to eat at the school as a guest (I haven't achieved VIP status yet) and am rarely disappointed by the fare on offer from either 'Gordon Ramsay's' team in the main dining hall or from the girls in the sixth form common room.

As a footnote to this chapter, I made it one of my aims on retirement to learn how to cook. I fulfilled most of my other plans quite quickly, but was not a 'natural' in the kitchen, which made it well over a year or so before I addressed this ambition.

The problem with my very occasional previous efforts was not only natural ability, but also a problem with timing if a number of pots etc. were required for a particular dish. I remember one particular afternoon, which should have resulted in a Thai green curry being on the plate in about thirty minutes.

I was still struggling after an hour after overcooking the pak choi and was beginning to panic about ever bringing anything to a plate when my ten-year-old grandson Alex came to the rescue and the family was eventually well fed about an hour later than planned.

And then I was given a book of 101 one-pot recipes.

At first I just put this on the shelf expecting the dishes to be too simple and uninteresting, but an eventual closer inspection revealed some interesting and varied dishes that I might be able to produce without calling for International Rescue.

And so I have found my culinary niche. Put simply, if it is all in one pot in front of me there is about a seventy-five per cent chance that I will succeed in producing a reasonable meal.

They don't, however, compare with school dinners!

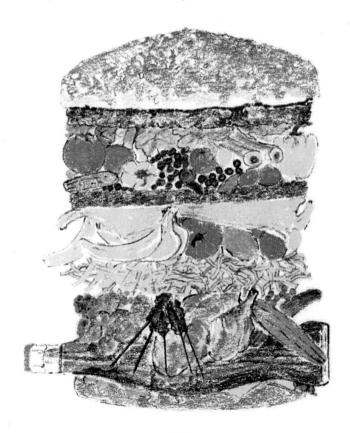

The Cock House Cup

Which yearly event at my third school aroused such varied emotions as pride, hysteria, boredom, hilarity, anger, hate and passion? Without a doubt, The Inter House Sports Competition, 'The Cock House Cup', or Cock-Up Cup as it was sometimes referred to by some members of staff (although obviously not during my reign as P.E. 'Supremo').

The origins of the competition dated back to the early part of the twentieth century when Quernmore School was a completely different set-up, more akin to the private sector, and the house system was the norm in most schools at the time. The house names reflected the spirit of battle and war, being famous World War Two generals, Montgomery, Alexander, Tedder and Cunningham, a fact that was rarely explained to any bemused new pupil on entering the school, one irate head of house even giving a pupil a detention on one occasion for 'not knowing his history'! Some of the plans hatched to win this historic crown made Watergate seem like an episode of *Blue Peter*. House masters were transformed into the likes of Genghis Khan and Napoleon, leading their elite forces into battle against the enemy. In the middle was the poor soul who had to organise and coordinate the series of events, the head of P.E., hiding away as much as possible to avoid possible bribes, threats, or proposed rule changes intended to suit one team or another and trying to be as impartial as possible. On the outside were those who were not interested in sport, or teachers upset at an alteration to their timetable to accommodate some silly selection event, a house assembly to rally the troops, or the competitions proper.

The trophy itself resembled a medieval wooden drinking mug which was the proud work of the school's long standing woodwork teacher, a real character and keen cricketer, who always exuded class in the annual staff v. pupils match...On one occasion, the staff were really struggling during their innings when he strode out purposefully to the centre in his somewhat ancient cricket gear. One spectating pupil close to me, already salivating at the demise of the teachers, suddenly announced, 'They must be struggling if they had to dig up W.G. Grace!' I complimented him on his cricketing knowledge, which was lost on most around him, but added that he may be in for a surprise. About an hour later after many glorious shots against both spin and speed I suggested that as our total was insurmountable our hero gave a catch to a pupil who was not one of the stars of the team and would get some recognition if he managed to hold on to the ball – which he duly did as it was deliberately hit straight to him and very softly.

But back to the trophy, which was about nine inches high and probably heavily polished walnut and an accomplished piece of woodwork. The problem was that the individual trophies for the various competitions literally outshone the main prize. Still, history could not be ignored and the combined totals of the yearly competitions resulted in a presentation ceremony complete with applause, raspberries and a prolonged speech from yours truly remembering the memorable individual and group performances from the year's competitions... and all slept well. In the weeks leading up to this 'celebration' a popular detention task would be to shine up the cups ready for the big day, so much so that the appearance of one of these trophies even brought the occasional admiring comment from the watching hordes... to be followed by a slightly puzzled murmur as The Cock House Cup was presented. My many attempts to explain the historical importance and tradition behind the cup being of more importance than its shine or size to pupils rarely met with success, even when I used a comparison with the Ashes.

The following pages contain some of my favourite moments from my ten or so years involvement with The Cock House Cup.

Great moments in sport (1)

The Cock- House Cup Senior Cross-Country event 1980 (Course chart on next page)

Being close to downtown Bromley, we were not blessed with nearby woods or fields. It was also considered too risky to march the whole school to a suitable 'green' venue as the senior staff were worried about losing half of the spectators on the way! The cross-country course was, therefore, partly round the school huts and buildings and then stretched out around the perimeter of the school playing field. Two laps was the distance for seniors, although one year the head of Tedder House approached me with the suggestion that the distance should be doubled. I was rightly suspicious and found out later that he had a very talented runner who excelled at the suggested longer distance. Unfortunately the accompanying bribe was only a cup of coffee and no money, so I stuck with the original format.

At the start the gun refused to fire but did so during a subsequent close inspection by yours truly, which I am sure is at least partly responsible for my poor hearing in later life. Being a freezing winter's day the runners were only too glad to set off at the earliest opportunity but were waved back by a frantic and temporarily deaf P.F.

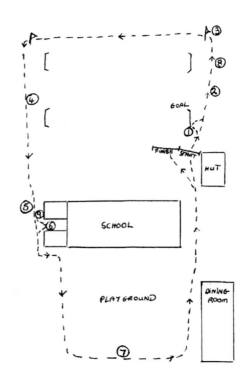

The second attempt at a start was successful gun-wise but an early injury was sustained by a boy too busy waving to his admiring fans to notice an approaching goal post (incident 1 on course chart). His nose was bloody, but not broken and he bravely continued after treatment from two members of staff, eventually finishing in the middle of the field. I manfully refused a request from the head of his house (Alexander) to start the race again as I knew that this was prompted by the runner being one of the pre-race favourites rather than any breach of the rules.

Some deliberate tripping by the resident school bully (incident 2) resulted in another favourite losing an early good position, but the objection raised by the head of his house (Montgomery) was turned down by P.F. as I had not seen the incident due to the need for a warming cup of coffee from the canteen (well, it was pretty cold for those not running!).

Some bunching at the front at the tight first turn (3) did not prove as dangerous as some had predicted on this first lap, possibly due to the fact that one of the runners had deliberately knocked down the marker flag and a subsequent runner placed it about ten feet away, substantially enlarging the turning area and slightly reducing the course distance.

By point 4, the heavy smokers were beginning to show at the back, one poor fellow being reduced to a crawl on all fours, accompanied by a desperate bout of coughing for a few desperate moments, until his nearby housemaster (Montgomery again) threatened him sufficiently to encourage him back to his feet and an eventual second to last result.

The strong favourite who had been tripped earlier had by now (5) re-established himself in the leading group and the race was beginning to settle down when suddenly the first six or seven who had broken away almost stopped dead, having been directed the wrong way (6) by a member of staff who had such an authoritarian nature that for a few seconds he was insisting they went in 'his' direction, despite the fact that this led to a dead end. Loud hailer at the ready an unusually alert P.F. urged the lads back on to the correct route just in time to stay ahead of the pack. The teacher, however, stormed off on strike announcing that I had made him look silly in front of the school.

The trek around the playground(7) proved relatively uneventful apart from a few slipping due to inappropriate footwear (i.e. football boots), but only a few cuts were subsequently reported ... End of lap one.

Lap two

The field had become quite strung out by now with most of the expected favourites in the leading group. Noticing his main hope was breathing rather heavily, the head of Alexander House decided to try and run alongside him giving a combination of verbal encouragement and threats. This unfortunately led to a collision between the head of Cunningham and himself(8). For one awful moment I thought we were in for a fight, but the head of Alexander was more concerned with the race and after a couple of token shoves, proceeded to try to catch up with his runner. The other heads of house obviously decided to follow suit and the spectators were presented with the comical site of some rather unfit gesticulating and shouting adults trying to keep up with the runners. After about 200 metres they gave up and took the short cut to the finish.

Meanwhile, the race was reaching its climax. There were no further major incidents until about three-quarters of the way round the field, when the strongest runner (Montgomery) started to open a significant gap. The head of Montgomery looked over towards me with a huge smile and exaggerated wink as a glorious result seemed assured. A ripple of applause from the Montgomery spectators, grew into a loud and confident symphony as he approached the school buildings for the last time(9) ... when suddenly he was showered from above with a mixture of gravy, half eaten vegetables and various other leftovers from that day's school lunch. Looking up at the window with considerable anger he saw two unidentified sixth formers hanging out of their common room with the slop bowl in hand. They quickly retreated before they could be identified and having witnessed the whole scene I attempted to convince the runner to carry on as he was still ahead and was sure to win. He looked at me, the crowd fell into a hush as he considered this proposal for a few seconds, before rushing into the school building in a vain attempt to dish out revenge on his attackers, who had fled the scene and were never identified (possibly due to the unwritten code of conduct that existed amongst the boys not to 'rat' on anyone). The instigators of the crime knew that the runner was well known for his fiery temper and that this was the only way to ensure that he didn't win! Or perhaps they were just 'having a laugh'. Anyway the race continued with the best Alexander runner eventually taking the title with a somewhat muted celebration. Noting the head of

Montgomery in a heated conversation with the head-master I attempted to beat a hasty retreat from any objections to the result by moving to the field to super-vise the collection of the marker flags, but was soon tapped on the shoulder by an irate head of Montgomery who wanted his runner re-instated as the winner. I pointed out that I could not do this as it was not another runner who had carried out the 'atrocity' and that I had told him to run on as it was only his pride that had been hurt. He didn't speak to me for weeks but eventually came to see my point of view. Perhaps the fact that Montgomery still managed to win the cup at the end of the year also soothed his temper...

The cross country was allowed to continue the following year with a member of staff strategically placed in the sixth form common room. Never again was there such excitement!

Great moments in sport (2)

Irish Olympics

My Irish friends are going to hate me for joining the 'Irish joke' bandwagon, but there is potential offered by the groundsman at Quernmore. The climax to the Cock House Cup was sports day and in 1980 it coincided with a few bloomers by Sean with regard to the set- up of the athletic track (he was a great guy just having a bad week).

Note: I have decided that this story is best suited to a diagrammatic approach, thus knocking on the head the idea that a P.E. teacher's technical expertise rarely extends beyond pumping up footballs.

Sports Day track marking 1980

Phase 1: Inspired by a new diagram from head office Sean set to work. This phase was aborted after the first lane was marked.

Key:

S = spectator area

⅔ =two thirds of a one lane 300m track

C= central measuring point

>= runners direction

27= garden of 27 London Lane

-- = school field boundary

F = finish line

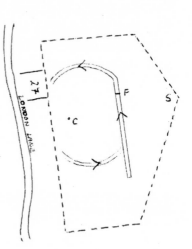

Comments

Advantages:

(1) Keen athletic followers at no. 27 London Lane offered a superb view of runners on back straight.
(2) Half a track is a saving on marking materials.

Disadvantages:

(1) Finish Line too far from spectators.
(2) Top fence at no. 27 made of barbed wire.
(3) Only 100 metres possible to complete.

Phase 2: This time six lanes were completed before a problem was noticed.

Additions to previous key:

P = pole vault run-up and sand pit

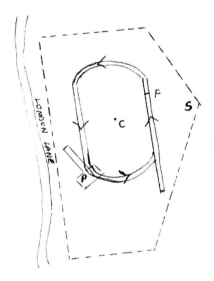

Advantages:

(1) Complete track now present
(2) Bend passing through sand provides good stamina training

Disadvantages:

(1) Regular raking between each race is required.
(2) No school records would be broken in any event requiring a run through the sand.

Phase 3: The positioning of the track was perfect at this stage, but in 1980 we had an excellent javelin thrower whose potential distance necessitated a move of the usual javelin throwing area to avoid the possibility of a neighbouring gardener being 'skewered'. Sean came up with the following solution.

n.b. It should be mentioned that the javelin event ran at the same time as certain track events.

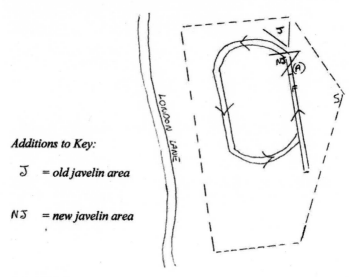

Additions to Key:

J = *old javelin area*

NJ = *new javelin area*

Advantages:

(1) Gardeners in neighbouring house safe.
(2) Tactical awareness of runners on bend (a) heightened by presence of sharp flying objects.

Disadvantages:

(1) Any runner hit would have resulted in a potentially difficult ruling for the track judge … me!
(2) A similar problem would have resulted if a track athlete had been tripped by a measuring tape.
(3) A really long throw would have 'spiked' the cricket square where I regularly practised my putting.

Postscript

The rain of the next few days fortunately washed out the javelin markings, but also most of the track! Sports day was postponed and by the time the sun had returned the grass was too long to be marked and a dispute between P.F. and the Borough gang mower driver who was refusing to cut our grass further hindered progress. The driver had tried to run down a whole P.E. class about a week before the 'serious' marking had started as he thought we shouldn't have been on the field at the time. I then staged a sit-down protest with the next class in the path of the murderous blades, which thankfully ground to a halt and departed ...(health and safety...ouch!) Pressure from 'higher up' resulted in a compromise on both sides and sports day arrived later than ever before with the track spread out in perfect majesty... or so I thought.

The weather was perfect and my organisation fine-tuned ... We had had the javelin competition a day earlier (to save lives) and after the usual welcome to parents etc. I was able to announce that, even before sports day had begun, a school and district record had been broken by our javelin superstar. I applied my factor ten suntan lotion, being already well bronzed from an unusually warm early summer and sat back to enjoy the proceedings, which went remarkably smoothly. So much so that I was able to stroll amongst the gathered hordes and accept their kind comments about organisation and the appearance of the boys etc. My good mood was further enhanced by the number of school records that were being broken on the track. A thumbs-up at distance from the headmaster almost carried me into a land of bliss ... but I was about to come crashing down to earth.

The first indication that something was wrong was when a fairly mediocre runner won the first year 200m, pushing the hot favourite into second place. There was a little murmuring and scratching of heads, but events moved on. I moved my attention away from the high jump for a moment to notice that another fairly average runner in lane one had won the third year 200m and with a new school record. During a break in proceedings a head of house came over to me and expressed his surprise that his 'superstar' had been defeated. As he left he made a passing comment about the track markings probably being wrong. I decided to check this as my suspicions had been aroused. As I moved over to the start of the fourth year 200m I soon realised with horror what was happening. The starting line for lane one instead of following the 'stagger' from lane two had actually been marked quite close to lane two, giving any runner in that lane a huge advantage. Amazingly, no one had made a complaint, or even brought it to my attention. I watched in horror as yet another school record was shattered by a very surprised runner and murmurs about secret training sessions and drugging were beginning to surface as I passed teachers and parents who were actually so far from the start line for the 'offending' races that they probably couldn't see who was in the inside lane at the start. I decided to take matters into my own hands by suggesting to the starter that he took a break and I took over for the remaining races. I knew that he didn't really want the job anyway, so he was grateful for this reprieve and sloped off to the refreshment area. I calculated the correct starting point for the remaining races and no one noticed a change. The school records, however, unfortunately dried up.

At the end of proceedings I expected a backlash, but apart from a few puzzled losers discussing some surprise results with their housemasters, the track marking error seemed to have gone unnoticed. I did intervene in one argument to point out to the head of Cunningham, who was considering punishing one of his team, that although his runner had only come second he had achieved a personal best time and that the winner had surprised us all and must have really trained hard to improve so much!

With an uneasy heart I collected the final result, which was always a tense moment as it inevitably arrived late, causing the school day to overrun by up to twenty minutes. With the headmaster checking his watch in a slightly agitated state I was eventually given the result. A close-run thing, but a win for Tedder for the first time in seven years. A quick glance at the results sheet revealed my worst fears, that Tedder had won a number of races from lane one against seemingly superior runners. The head of Tedder was giving a congratulatory speech to my left as I contemplated what to do.

It was traditional for the head of P.E. to check the results before any final announcement, but as we were running late the headmaster grabbed the sheet from me and proceeded to announce the winning house and say all the usual 'thank you's and 'well done's. I cringed, but forced a smile, when he suggested that the plethora of school records this year was due to the excellent athletic lessons and training and then proceeded to 'tidy up' as the parents, teachers and pupils left. About an hour later I was still contemplating coming clean about the track and working out who I should tell, as I glanced at the result sheets. To my horror the result was wrong, with a mistaken total for Tedder pushing them from second to first. This was probably due to the headmaster pressurising the scorekeepers as we were running late, or perhaps a faulty calculator.

The next morning I trudged along to the head's office with the double whammy of bad news. It had been a difficult few weeks at school with some bad pupil behaviour and staff illness, so I was not relishing the thought of introducing some serious problems with an event that had seemed to go so well. I was greeted cheerfully and then praised for my organisation and the pupils' performances before the head relaxed into his easy chair, lit his pipe and proceeded to gaze out at the school field with a satisfied air. This was usually the sign that a meeting was over, so when I remained in my seat, the head announced, 'Is there anything else, Peter?'

I was momentarily tempted to make a leaving comment and get up, but then told him the sorry truths about the track marking, incorrect records and wrong result. He thought for about fifteen seconds before swivelling round towards me and announcing, 'Peter, that was the best sports day we have ever had. The number of records was terrific and it was great that Tedder won after so many years in the wilderness; and very well done on the organisation.' As these final words came out he gestured to me to pass him the results sheets which I had brought along as 'evidence', tore them up slowly and placed the pieces carefully in a bin, then looked me straight in the eye and said, 'I am really looking forward to the summer Peter, I need to relax after a difficult year.' The look on his face made it clear that the sports day mistakes were never to be mentioned again. He did agree the following year, however, that it was OK if sports day ran a few minutes late, in order to ensure that the scorers produced the right result!

School Trips

The nightmare actually starts as a pleasant dream...

It is a lovely spring day in the Lake District. A group of about twenty schoolchildren (including me) are winding their way up a valley towards a distant peak.

The conversation is bubbling along nicely, and includes the usual teenage stuff like who fancies who and how many beers did you manage to secretly drink the night before?

Even the teachers seem to be in a fine mood, perhaps as a result of our good behaviour on the trip so far (at least on the surface).

As we rise a little further up the valley we are asked to put our jackets on and there are a few murmurs of disapproval as it is still so pleasantly warm. But our leader (geography teacher) insists that the temperature will soon drop and backs this up with some impressive statistical knowledge about height gained and temperature dropped.

At about 1,500ft it does indeed start to get colder and an unpleasant drizzle starts to fall. It soon becomes heavy rainfall and yet as I turn round I can still see the lower valley bathed in sunshine. A few are heard to mumble requests to turn back, but our leader is made of sterner stuff and probably relishes these more difficult conditions.

We all begin to form a line so that the body in front gives a little protection from the strong wind and even heavier rain.

And then there is a halt.

Somewhere in front of me I can hear a teacher describing the next part of the walk as 'tricky, especially in the slippery conditions' and that we need to be 'sensible' and 'not look down'.

I nudge my way forward and see a knife-edge ridge (arête, if you're a geographer) with sheer drops of at least a thousand feet on either side and a path almost on top of the ridge that gives the impression that if you had one foot on the path, the only place for the other one is on the other side!

We start off and although the path is wider than it looked at a distance, it is still possible to lean over and look down the drop on the other side.

The wind is even stronger on this exposed section and all these factors combine to bring forth two or three strong protests from the pupils, which are shot down by the group leader. 'This is what we came for! You can't expect good weather and flat paths in the Lake District!' His eyes glint with excitement as he finishes this sentence and as if on cue the rain turns to sleet. Is all this weather possible in April?

Despite our leader's sound advice it is almost impossible not to look down and be terrified by the drop. A few of the boys and girls are even down on all fours, frightened of being blown over in a more upright position (I take this option on one or two tricky sections).

And then a boy slips!

I see him fall and hear the screams of other pupils. I can see his hands clinging onto a rock and realise thankfully that he is on a wider section and was not in any danger of going over the edge.

This does, however, unnerve another boy and girl who start to shake all over and begin a sit-down strike, which takes all of ten minutes to resolve before we move on again. (The group leader threatened to leave them and go on if they refused to stand up, but possibly realising his attitude was a trifle harsh added with a gentler voice that they could reposition themselves directly behind him.) By now a state of semi-hysteria has afflicted at least half a dozen, who all adopt 'the crawl' and move at an achingly slow pace.

We are well over 2,500 feet now and those with inferior or insufficient waterproof and windproof clothing are starting to shiver; and then the rain turns to snow. At first it is fairly light and as the clouds part for a moment I can see that the ridge ends after another fifty foot and a wide path seems to snake up a fairly modest gradient. 'Soon be at the top!' shouts the leader and our spirits are lifted as the ridge fades into the distance.

Twenty minutes later and we are walking almost on level ground.

Suddenly, as if blown by a giant, a rush of denser snow sweeps across our group, which in a few minutes brings visibility down to about twenty feet.

The shivering is increasing and some thermal blankets are handed out to the worst victims. These are almost useless as they are being blown all over the place as we are still moving around.

A few minutes pass and then the leader shouts out in triumph that we have reached the summit! This is small consolation for most of the children who just want to escape from 'hell'…and the weather takes a final turn for the worse as the thick, wind driven snow becomes a 'white out' with visibility down to only a few feet.

Perhaps finally realising the perilous nature of the predicament, the three teachers gather closely together for a conference, instructing us to 'get in a huddle together' and 'on no account walk off as there could be some cliff edges nearby, invisible due to the snow.'

This produces a spontaneous and loud moan from all the children, who huddle so close together that under different circumstances it could be construed that at least six new relationships had suddenly sprung up!

After five minutes 'cuddling' and shivering the teachers return with the announcement that four selected pupils would be sent in different directions to find 'the safe route down'. Although fairly sure of the correct direction it has been decided to send out scouts to locate a secondary cairn (pile of rocks) that would indicate the beginning of the safe downward path.

I feel a shiver going through my previously quite warm body as I am 'selected' and feel like shouting

'Shouldn't we be asking for volunteers?' but one part of me is quietly pleased that I have been selected for this dangerous mission, and the other half doesn't want to be shown up in front of the girls, so I head off gingerly in the direction I have been told.

My progress is very slow as I have visions of walking off the edge of one of the highest mountains in England ...and I can hardly see my feet! After a few steps a quick glance back also scares me as I can't see any other living thing!

I decide that the best plan is to make exaggerated footprints in the snow to help retrace my steps and I murmur words of encouragement to myself as well as hoping that a shout will mean that one of the other brave explorers has found the correct path and I can return ...

So far this dream, which turns into a nightmare, is actually true. I hate to think what today's health and safety brigade would have to say about this!

For some reason this recurring dream of mine then moves off into a bizarre series of events ...

I am trudging on slowly and becoming so afraid that I turn around and decide to go back, but as I do so a terrifying vision appears before me. It is the teacher leading the group, but twice his normal size and with a grotesque face, similar to a human half changed into a werewolf. His eyes come alight with a powerful blue ray that stops me in my tracks and then as a swirl of snow covers him up a hairy arm points in the direction I should be going.

There is no resisting this fearful vision, so I turn again, take a few short steps and then feel the snow fall away beneath my feet. I tumble through space, only to come crashing to a halt on a ledge.

As I move from the edge backwards I come face-to-face with a golden eagle who jabs one of my eyes viciously with his beak, causing me to fall again.

This time the fall is longer and I am circled by a squawking eagle on my journey downwards. Suddenly, the air is crushed out of me as an arm reaches out from the cliff face to catch me. It is one of the nice teachers, Mr Jones (strong and P.E.) who has saved me, but just as I look at his reassuring smile he is transformed into a snarling Yeti, who throws me towards the edge of the ledge! I slither off the edge but manage to just hold on to the trunk of a small bush. I don't have the strength to pull myself up, but perhaps the P.E. teacher (If he's not a Yeti) will be able to do so if I just hang on long enough!

A stamp of feet towards me tells me this is not human and a hairy arm snaps the bush off the cliff leaving me falling … falling … falling.

This is when I usually wake up in a cold sweat!

I actually have been free from this dream/nightmare for some years now, and in real life we did eventually manage to not only find our way off the mountain, but also experienced the same sequence of weather conditions in reverse order.

Sometimes the dream would occur on the nights close to a school trip that I had organised, or if I was about to go on a holiday to the Scottish Highlands, or the Lake District. But other occurrences seemed quite random.

I'm sure that Sigmund Freud would have had a field day analysing my nightmare, but the truth is that most of my experiences of school trips have been good ones. Even the Lake District week was enjoyable apart from the day mentioned above, and I have fond memories of picking strawberries in Kent, playing on south coast beaches, as well as collecting shells etc, and even brass rubbing in musty Norman churches.

Being a member of the P.E. department and having an interest in outdoor pursuits, coupled with a desire to break up the routine of day-to-day teaching from time to time, meant that I organised a number of sport-based school trips during my teaching career.

I even, despite not being a particularly good skier, ran two school trips to Italy. The first of these was in a fairly small resort with little to do in the evening, which wasn't perfect, but a good time was had by all as we made our own entertainment to a certain extent.

During the actual skiing sessions the boys seemed to be divided into two clear groups; very good skiers, plus a few fearless quick learners, and a second group of beginners who, mostly through nerves, didn't progress that much throughout the week.

It seemed that I had moderate ability and I found myself in the top group, a situation I didn't really like.

Although far from expert at any water sport, I was quite happy to fall off a sailboard, capsize a dinghy, or be swallowed up by a large wave while surfing, because it usually ended up with a soft landing.

But speed on land was another matter, especially with two long objects attached to my ski boots just waiting to twist and break either a foot or leg!

My only skiing injury was actually a dislocated finger acquired during a weekend skiing course on a dry slope in England. I was standing at the top of the run waiting to descend slowly via a series of wide snow-plough turns, when a colleague took an unusual tumble on the slope below. She had been unable to slow down at the end of her run and ended up flattening the instructor, who had seen the danger too late!

After checking briefly that no one was hurt, I laughed so much that I lost my balance, fell over and dislocated a thumb in the matting of the artificial slope.

The two other teachers on the trip were both rugby players and suggested a no-nonsense approach to my injury involving one of them holding my arm firmly while the other manipulated the thumb back into position. I achieved wimp status by electing instead to visit the local hospital for what turned out to be painful, but professional, repairs.

Sledging was fine, as a tumble meant just a well-padded skid and a few laughs.

If only the instructors would have left me alone to float around in cable cars taking photos of the group, combined with stop-offs at the many Alpine cafés with fantastic scenery and views, I would have been happy. But no, I couldn't refuse to take part if one or two of the boys were also unsure, as this would set a bad example!

Imagine my glee when on the third day our instructors decided to create a third, middle ability group, who would ski on fairly moderate slopes, but not the black runs!

I volunteered to stay with this group, but my instructor (probably recognising my real intentions) insisted I stayed with the top group, in which I was easily the worst skier, and probably the most unhappy!

There was, however, the magnificent Alpine scenery and the company of other teachers to make the experience worthwile... and the trip wasn't for me anyway, but the kids!

The following year, we upgraded to Madesimo, a moderately-sized, but very attractive resort on the Italian/French border.

This not only had superior skiing, and an excellent network of 'doorstep' cable cars and lifts, but also good après ski facilities, including a skating rink, bowling alley and a number of teenage-friendly nightclubs where the group could let off steam.

Mike, Bea (expert Scottish skier and bonnie lass!) and I had taken a group of sixth-form boys with us that year and were hoping that they would be well behaved, as they were of an age where back home they would be allowed out to clubs, dances, etc. on a fairly regular basis, and yet we were responsible for their behaviour.

At the pre-trip briefing (attended also by parents) we had issued a 'no alcohol' and other rules, which we had expected to be at least mildly challenged, especially as some of the group were eighteen, but despite a few unhappy faces, contracts were signed and boundaries set without too much complaint.

There still remained the question of how to amuse the lads in the evening, but this was solved at the first morning gathering for breakfast, when in walked a bevy of gorgeous sixth-form girls from a school in Yorkshire.

To their credit, the boys played it cool for that first morning, gradually introducing themselves and indulging in acts of chivalry, such as bringing over a second cup of coffee to the girls' teachers, offering to take the girls' plates and cups over to the washing-up, or just chatting at the buffet-style breakfast table.

By the third morning however, there were boys and girls mixed together at all of the tables, and we had also made friends and were sitting with the husband and wife team of teachers from the other school.

We all found this teenage interaction highly amusing, but the conversation soon moved to how long it would be before the first request would come from a pupil to be allowed out 'alone' with someone from the other school, or something equally as dodgy.

But we had underestimated them.

It was the same day that we had prepared ourselves for the first problem as a special dance event ('70s or '80s style if I remember) was being advertised on posters around the resort and throughout the morning ski session the girls and boys were constantly making references to 'how good it sounded' and 'wouldn't it be great if we could go' within earshot of one of the teachers.

It was during a cappuccino break at the top of one of the local mountains (with a view to die for) that we were approached by one of the 'leaders' from our school and the head girl from the other.

As they approached we prepared ourselves for a difficult decision and how to best deliver a 'no' to sensible young adults.

The conversation went something like this...

Edward; 'Excuse me for interrupting but Jane and I wanted to put an idea to you all about this evening.'

Jane; 'Yes, we've had a meeting with all the boys and girls and everyone would love to go to the dance tonight in town. The thing is we feel a bit worried about going alone, so we wondered if you would mind coming to look after us?'

Edward; 'It wouldn't be too late because we obviously need a good night's sleep before all the skiing tomorrow ... Also, we want you to have an enjoyable evening so perhaps Miss (the other teacher's wife) wouldn't mind having one or two dances with Mr Foster and Mr Clark; I've seen them dance and they're both really good!' (This could have been a potential fatal mistake as Mike hates dancing, and I am willing, but useless!)

Jane; 'We also met the owner of the club (how did she manage that?) and he told us that if we brought thirty or more people, plus teachers, then the teachers would have free drinks.'

Edward; 'We realise that this is a big ask but I am sure that everyone would really appreciate it if we could go, and we promise to behave ourselves.'

Jane; 'Oh, and we're not trying to bribe you with drink. We know that none of you drink much, being responsible teachers ... so please have soft drinks if you prefer.'

We all had a really fun evening at the disco, with yours truly leading the line dancing, the boys and girls behaving impeccably, and the teachers from both schools able to relax in the face of a constant charm offensive from both the boys and girls. We had constant waiter and snack service from the girls and boys, who also took the time to come and chat with us throughout the evening. There was even a rota of girls arranged who pretended to be 'dying' to have a dance with the male teachers.

On subsequent evenings, we enjoyed skating and bowling evenings with some of the nicest young ladies and gentleman you could ever wish to meet. If something 'naughty' had been going on we certainly didn't notice it; even my nightly room checks, cleverly arranged at different times did not reveal anything untoward!

The final evening included a sledging race, with a boy and girl on each sledge of course, followed by an Italian meal at a local restaurant with the teacher's tabs covered by a 'whip round' suggested and organised by the two groups of students.

As it was the last night we (teachers included) were all allowed to stay up late for the final event, a talent show organised (you guessed it) by the boys and girls.

I had managed to borrow an Elvis wig and sunglasses from one of the local gift shops and gyrated to 'Burning Love' for a few minutes. The lady teacher from the other school had real singing ability and gave us two of the Carpenters' biggest hits, while her husband had a talent for juggling with glasses, which was both a novelty and very well performed.

The boys and girls also came up trumps with some great singing and dancing as well as one or two hilarious impersonations of their teachers' mannerisms and catch phrases.

It was at this event that a mystery that had been puzzling me was also cleared up...

Not being a real skier I had borrowed some clothing from a friend of roughly the same build and I thought I was cutting quiet a dashing figure in my bright red one-piece suit, with white bobble hat and matching glasses ... yet when I appeared every day I was always greeted by a lot of whispering, followed by 'the giggles'.

I couldn't figure out what the joke was and most days just checked that my zip wasn't undone and that I didn't have a note stuck to my back saying 'rubbish skier' or the like and then forgot about it ... but as the laughter increased I began to get a little worried, so I decided to ask one or two carefully selected individuals if there was anything about me that was causing mirth. The reply was always in the negative, but my suspicions were raised even further when arch prankster Mike was with me when I was asking one of our group and was trying desperately to hide a laugh with a couple of vigorous coughs.

Anyway, at the end of the 'show' the teachers from both schools were given thank you presents. Mike received a disco album to help him with his dancing, Bea received a 'Learn how to speak English' book and I was handed a poster promoting safe sex! It was then explained to me that in my red suit and white hat I looked very similar to 'Captain Condom'!

One of the highlights of the trip was the afternoon when you could choose an alternative activity to skiing.

As the boys and girls were all being supervised by instructors we were told to choose anything we liked. Both Mike and I had been impressed by the individuals and groups we had seen throughout the week on Skidoos (powered sledges) and had this at joint top of our list competing with snowboarding, which I was sure I would be better at than skiing due to a few years' surfing down in Cornwall.

We chose snowboarding as we weren't sure if we would only be allowed to be passengers on a Skidoo, and after a basic safety and technique talk, Mike and I were ready to go.

Mike had a tendency to not bother too much about technique and just aim whatever was attached to his feet straight downhill and set off.

This often resulted in some impressive speeds, but potentially dangerous situations, as both slowing down and turning were alien to him. The instructor who was with us most days nicknamed him 'Crazy Mico' and had to relegate him to some gentler slopes that didn't end in a cliff edge!

It was the same instructor who was taking about seven of us on this snowboarding afternoon.

The first two students and teacher all had very impressive runs and then it was Mike's turn. I feared the worst when he told everyone in a direct path downhill to move out of the way, and the instructor also recognised what was about to happen and rushed up to Mike and supported him on a couple of zigzags across, rather than down the slope.

Although Mike fell over a couple of times, I felt sure that he had got the message by the time he was ready for his first solo run.

It started well and Mike moved slowly across the slope to some generous and encouraging applause. Gradually, however, gravity began to take over and he began to turn straight downhill and increase in speed.

This unfortunately coincided with the steepest part of the slope and within seconds Mike was hurtling towards a group of innocent Italians enjoying a combination of sun and cappuccino.

He shouted a warning and thankfully they all managed to leap to one side! Mike meanwhile had remained upright for a remarkably long period of time and was fast approaching the entrance to a café!

At the last moment he decided to bail out sideways and ended up in a heap, covered in snow at the feet of some expert skiers who found the whole thing very amusing (after checking he wasn't injured) and warmly applauded the 'show'.

The instructor turned to me and said in a voice similar to Manuel in *Fawlty Towers*, 'I told you, this Mico, he crazy!'.

We were standing at the top of a mound with steep sides in all directions. I found Mike's performance so funny that I started to rock with laughter, which resulted in me sliding off the mound in an unscheduled fast backward slide that was only halted when I crashed into a tree!

Although winded, I was unhurt, but Mike got the final laugh by asking me to 'show the group that advanced move again'.

As an aside, this was not the best crash of the week. It was possibly this one...

A few days after the snowboarding we were taking our morning break on a gloriously sunny day that was so warm I was even down to my T-shirt.

The cold drink had gone down a treat and I had about another thirty minutes relaxation time before the skiing started again, which was great as I had managed to grab one of the very comfortable deckchairs.

I was just dropping off when a loud and ladylike scream broke the peace. It was an Italian lady who had panicked on the nursery slope and found herself heading at an ever-increasing speed (à la Mico) towards the cable car station.

I was (surprisingly) the first to react and rushed out into her path. Not knowing her nationality at that moment I signalled for her to come straight at me but throw away her poles.

The poles were thrown away, but my planned rugby-style tackle was in jeopardy as she swerved at the last moment. I leaped to the same side, but she veered back and seeing she was going to hit me attempted an emergency snow plough stop with arms out in front to brace any impact ... which resulted in her catapulting into my arms with a leg either side of me. I instinctively fell backwards to cushion the impact and we ended up in a compromising position with me flat on my back and her astride and on top!

After checking she was OK and establishing from the answer that she was Italian, I turned to the café where there had been a spontaneous round of applause and shouted, 'Wow! These Italian girls don't mess about, do they!'

Or was it this one?

There hadn't been any fresh snowfall by the fifth day and the warm day-time temperatures combined with the night-time freeze had created very icy conditions.

Our instructors had been sensible in downgrading the runs we were going to attempt, which suited me fine until I found myself at the foot of a very steep drag lift that was even icier than the actual runs.

I was quite confident on drag lifts but had been known to take an occasional fall if I let my concentration slip.

Mike was to join the lift two or three spots behind me and was looking for any excuse to get out of skiing, which he eventually succeeded in doing by announcing that this was the perfect place to get some group and individual photographs of the boys in action. It was with a sly wink to me that he took his skis off and retrieved his camera.

A few minutes later I was halfway up the lift when I heard some shouting above me.

Mike was waving to me from a chairlift that crossed over the top of ours. How he had timed this photo opportunity so well was beyond me (just luck perhaps) but he shouted at me to smile.

I was so intent on adopting a cool pose that I leant over a bit too far and fell off the 'button'.

I started to accelerate downhill flat on my front and straight at the next person below me on the lift. The lift had been stopped and the man below me took impressive evasive action by swinging out to one side.

Unfortunately my speed on the sheet ice was increasing at such a rate that I crashed into and through the next three unfortunates on the lift.

Before I killed someone I managed to dig a ski into the ice and veer to one side before coming slowly to a stop.

As I looked back up the slope at the carnage, to my relief no one seemed to be injured and on closer inspection this proved to be the case. I was, however, banned from the lift for the rest of the day!

No, I think this was the best one!

On the snowboarding day, Mike and I eventually managed some reasonable attempts, but I had to concede that the skill transference from surfing to snow-boarding was not as simple as I had thought.

So as we walked away from the instruction area there was a certain amount of frustration that we hadn't chosen to have a go on a Skidoo.

We looked across to the Skidoo station and noticed a group, including some of our lads, about to set off, and then almost simultaneously we noticed a spare Skidoo!

I looked at Mike, he looked at me and nothing needed to be said ... after a little bit of pleading we were allowed to use the last vehicle. Cue high fives!

The others were a little peeved at the subsequent delay as we needed to hear some basic pieces of instruction, which included;

'Use plenty of throttle to get started as you are heavy',

'Stay close to the leader as the snowfall is going to get big',

'If anything goes wrong, jump clear of the Skidoo... they are heavy!'

The instructor then assured us that there was no danger if we all stayed close as the track was in fact quite wide.

Mike is very good at following instructions to the letter, but as we started off his 'plenty of throttle' caused the machine to leap forward tipping me off the back in a perfect backward somersault (the only one I have ever completed).

I was however unhurt and we set off again, this time with me holding on tightly to Mike (it should have been a girl).

After a few bumpy moments our progress became quite serene and as well as complementing Mike on his driving, I was able to relax and take in the lovely scenery.

I could see the winding track ahead and became quite excited when I noticed it seemed to be heading up towards a renowned viewpoint. Mike had also become quite proficient and he told me he was going to drop behind a few times so that we could put in a good burst of speed, which, despite my dislike of speed on land, I actually found quite exhilarating!

The light snow that had accompanied the start of the trip had by now turned into quite thick stuff and it became more difficult to not only keep up with the others but also see the path.

Our instructor stopped and gave us the option of going back or moving at a slower pace in a tighter unit. We were all enjoying the experience so much that despite the deteriorating conditions, the vote was unanimous to continue.

Off we went again and although the views were gone, there was an increased excitement level with the reduced visibility and snow rushing past!

A few minutes later it was becoming a blizzard.

Mike was having a little trouble keeping up as he didn't want to bash into the rear of the Skidoo in front ... and then on a winding steep section he slowed a little too much ... so much so that we stalled.

I could see the others disappearing into the snow and urged Mike to catch up. He got the message and after quickly restarting put in an impressive burst of speed. I shouted that I couldn't see the others and so Mike opened the throttle even more.

The next moment we were in mid air as Mike had missed an elevated turn to the left. He jumped clear, but I was strangely fascinated by this quiet moment as the engine cut out and I momentarily floated in space.

I was rudely awakened but unhurt as the Skidoo landed just short of a chalet ground-floor window. Inside were a family seated round their dinner table. A man and a woman got out of their chairs and I gave an embarrassed wave to them as they peered out towards me.

Having decided that I was not mad or trying to break in, they kindly helped Mike and I push the Skidoo back onto the track where the convoy had returned to discover our fate. The instructor was relieved that we were not hurt but even more so that the Skidoo had escaped without even a scratch!

There were a number of other foreign trips that I either organised or was asked to go on, and I have fond memories of football in Germany and a cultural visit to Finland, to name just two.

I also organised a water sports holiday in the south of France which was particularly interesting for Mike as he was keen to point out to me a year before we went on this trip, that the company who ran the trip offered a week's free preview to one teacher from each school provided that the preview was then followed up with a paying group of at least twenty within twelve months of the 'freebie'.

Well, we had already decided to take a group the following summer and had received permission from the school, so why not take advantage of this offer, with the added bonus of Mike being able to check out the dos and don'ts etc. for the following year.

His research did indeed make our subsequent trip all the more enjoyable, but Mike also had one or two interesting personal experiences on his preview week!

He was (and is) the type who is always keen to try something new, and waterskiing was top of his list that week!

The instructor had told him to keep his arms straight and one or two other points to help rise smoothly out of the water into a standing position.

After two or three runs and some fairly hefty crashes, Mike had still not got 'above water' and so the instructor took him aside and after running through the essentials one more time, decided he warranted one final try.

As the motor-boat set off Mike was battered but in a determined mood!

The motor speeded up but he didn't seem to be rising up correctly. So he leant back more and held on for dear life!

By this time his head was almost in the water, but the effect of the spray from his efforts to stand up was so strong that he was experiencing a sharp, and constant, rush of water into his mouth, which then gushed out of his nostrils ... but still he would not let go!

Eventually the boat stopped as Mike had not taken a breath for at least fifteen seconds... and Mike lived to try another activity, Scuba diving.

The instruction for this was worryingly basic and hampered by the instructor's lack of basic English (or Mike's inability to speak French if you want to see it from that way round), but the smiling faces of the other learners and the fact that he could see the sea bottom from their moored boat encouraged Mike to have a go anyway. He had learnt some safety signals for 'the deep' and had also grasped that if any water entered his mouth he was to blow out in his mouthpiece and it would be expelled through a valve.

The lesson began without any major incidents, apart from some mild earache, which Mike expected anyway as he had a slightly damaged eardrum from an infection when he was young.

Although slightly apprehensive, the presence of an experienced 'buddy' was also reassuring as they ventured a little deeper.

And then Mike accidentally took in some water.

He tapped his buddy and indicated the problem and that he wanted to surface. But the instructor held him down and proceeded to remind him through signals, how to eject the water.

Mike was becoming quiet agitated by now and was having difficulty breathing. He again signalled to go up.

The attempted calm reassurance again delivered by the instructor was by now being ignored. Mike broke free from his buddy's grip and in a mad dash for the surface proceeded to tramp all over his instructor's shoulder and face.

On breaking surface, Mike for an awful moment thought that he had done some real damage to his poor instructor, but he emerged alive, not in the best of moods, a few moments later.

My favourite school trips have to be our visits to Bowles Outdoor Centre, near Tunbridge Wells.

I had been looking for some time for a venue that would combine reasonable prices with a worthwhile introduction to a number of outdoor pursuits. It is quite amusing to think now that it took a five-year search, including trips to north Wales and visits to out-of-season Butlins camps, before I eventually was informed of this excellent centre practically on our doorstep! It had its own natural outcrop of sandstone, a ski slope and was set in beautiful countryside ideal for hiking and orienteering. There was also the added bonus of easy access to the river Medway or the Sussex coast for canoeing. The icing on the cake was the chalet accommodation, which was far more comfortable than anything we had experienced before, and certainly more welcoming than a wet tent.

There were also some amusing moments.

I must give Mike a 'rest' in a page or so but his efforts at abseiling are a good starting point...

If the climbing session had gone well and there was still a little time before the next meal the group would be given a chance to try abseiling.

On one of our trips to Bowles, Mike decided to have a go.

It is natural for an inexperienced abseiler to want to keep fairly upright and look down at their feet, but the trick is to actually lean quite a way back and then push out and bounce down the rock face. The more timid can also walk down effectively in this position.

If you stay too upright, your feet are constantly slipping and the head and arms consequently regularly clatter against the rock face.

Mike had taken the lean back quite literally and cut an impressive figure with a practically horizontal posture as he started to move downwards.

Unfortunately he then leant even further out and fell backwards, ending up upside-down and lying vertically against the rock.

The instructor was calmness personified and to those of us below, the scene was quite amusing. The situation, however, was complicated by the fact that Mike's climbing rope had somehow wrapped itself around his throat.

Despite our instructor's best attempts to coach him into a 'head up' position, he was unable to move because of the pressure of the rope forcing him against the rock face and was also having trouble breathing with the rope round his neck.

As the instructor couldn't let go at the top, another passing instructor took stock of the situation and also attempted to talk Mike to 'safety', but he still found it impossible to move.

It was eventually decided to let go of the rope that was trapping Mike and lower him slowly, head first, to the ground with the safety rope.

This didn't appeal to him particularly, and he took some persuading before agreeing that this was a better option than slow death through strangulation!

He was lowered down and supported by the shoulders until he reached safety, but it took him a good few minutes to recover, vowing never again to abseil!

Mobile pursuits

It was around 2007 that an unusual group asked to go on an outdoor pursuit weekend.

About ten of the year ten girls who 'signed up' were not exactly keen sportswomen at school and although their behaviour in general wasn't that bad, I wouldn't call them enthusiastic about anything, except make-up and boys!

I decided to consult a number of senior staff about their suitability before officially accepting them on the trip, and they also expressed surprise at the list, but couldn't find any reason to ban them from coming along.

It was decided to wait and see how they behaved at an introductory talk and film I was due to give in a few days, where I would emphasise a little earlier than usual the need for good behaviour, the ban on smoking and alcohol etc. and the need to stay on site at all times, to mention just a few of the rules.

I expected at least two of them to complain about some of these restrictions, but there wasn't a peep from any of them as I delivered my speech. I made a final comment about the requirement to be on time and take part enthusiastically in all the activities, but this was also meekly accepted by all present.

My final attempt to flush out their real reasons for going involved the sleeping arrangements.

Although we tried to keep friends together whenever possible, there were only four to a chalet room and the final decision on who would be with who was the teachers'. Surely they wouldn't like this if they just wanted a social weekend away, but again, not a sound!

I still had doubts about the girls' motives, but informed them that they had been accepted.

The trip down was fairly uneventful and the evening meal at about 6.30p.m. was enjoyed by all.

And then came the first activity bell for an evening on the ski slope.

All except six of the girls I have highlighted were ready to go in the ski chalet at least ten minutes before it sounded. At 6.30p.m. they had not arrived.

By about 6.35p.m. I asked the female teacher from our school to go and investigate why they were late. She found a scene reminiscent of a high street beauty salon in the girls' two rooms, where make-up was being applied, nails polished and suitable fragrances being discussed for the evening. They received a good telling-off and two received an extra warning as they had tried to insist on finishing their make-up rather than appear 'half done'! They eventually arrived fifteen minutes late. We also reminded them that the reason they had chosen to be here was to take part in outdoor pursuits and that a few days away from make-up and other 'luxuries' would probably do them good. They didn't seem that impressed.

The group was divided into the beginners and those who were more experienced and they were directed to either the easy or more difficult slopes. I had decided to move around on this first evening to observe how the whole group were doing and also to give everyone encouragement. The more advanced front slope group had one of my favourite instructors and were not only performing well, but having a good time, so I took a break from skiing and walked round the back to the 'nursery' slope where I was met by the sight of an angry instructor who was trying to get three of her group to stop texting their friends and family and resume skiing.

I stepped in, took the girls to one side and not only reminded them that one of the rules was 'no mobiles on during the activities', but also that they could not just decide to stop when they felt like it.

'But me mum told me to text her to say if I was all right.'

And 'We're knackered anyway – this is too hard!' were two of the inappropriate comments which ensued, so I had to not only read the riot act but also issue an extra duty punishment to the guilty parties.

This did not go down well, but at least they took part for the rest of the session.

The punishment was to relieve another school group of their dinner cleaning-up duty and anticipating a bit of 'anti' I decided to hang around after the meal to make sure they completed their task.

Just at that moment I was asked to go to the site office for a minute and requested to move one of our minibuses from its parking space before going to bed as it was slightly in the way of the canoe store which would need to be accessed early the next day.

I was only away a few minutes and on returning, found three girls chatting on their phones with one hand while either brushing or sweeping the same area over and over in a very casual and sloppy way with a brush or broom held in the other.

Phones were confiscated and punishments increased!

By now the girls were really fed up with life and one threatened to go home if I wasn't going to be more reasonable. I pointed out that their parents would have to come and collect them and that they wouldn't get a refund.

The crisis was temporarily averted … I was close to banning mobile phones completely but this would have been punishing the majority who were only using them during free time. A significant number of these didn't use their phone at all after the first evening as they were too busy enjoying themselves!

There were two final chapters to the phone saga.

After one more indiscretion I did eventually ban mobile phones being brought on any activity, but one young lady obviously had two as was revealed the next morning when I noticed a climbing rope looking far too slack.

The girl who was belaying another pupil on a quite challenging route, was not only using just one hand which made the process unsafe, but also not even watching the climber above!

She was banned from all activities for the rest of the day and this resulted in her friends sulking for the remainder of the trip. They were not allowed to go the following year and their behaviour was not typical of the vast majority of pupils I shared these 'adventures' with!

From a personal point of view, the school trips I attended allowed me to visit some great countries and also some of the loveliest parts of our own land. Although I never became particularly good at any outdoor pursuit, with the possible exception of canoeing, I have happy memories of activity-filled days and watching many pupils blossom into more confident youngsters during these trips (some students went on the Bowles trip every year of their time at the school). There were a number who surprised us with their ability and confidence, set free from the standard sporting activities that were on offer back at school.

The Good, The Bad and The Unteachable

It was Friday and Sam's last chance to be expelled that week, or 'permanently excluded' as it is called these days. I wonder why the 'powers that be' made this word change? Perhaps exclusion is slightly less harsh-sounding. But then to further complicate matters you have a number of exclusion levels including 'fixed term' and 'unspecified', before 'the chop' eventually comes. On reflection, I think the change is a politically correct one, similar in a way to the US Army referring to dead soldiers as 'inoperative personnel'.

Sam had been behaving outrageously all week and wanted to be kicked out of school, but he was highly intelligent and had something of the lovable rogue about him, so the general consensus was that he could succeed at school if he just found a constructive outlet for his energies sooner rather than later. How much more of his disruptive behaviour could be 'managed' without resorting to exclusion was also an issue as we didn't want other potentially disruptive pupils to believe that they could get away with anything. It had become very difficult to teach a class with Sam's constant interruptions and if he was removed to another room, he would create havoc or just simply walk out.

The real problem was twofold. Our education system just didn't have any appeal for Sam, he was going to run his own business when he left school, or if that didn't happen he had been promised a job in his dad's garage. I was his year head at the time and had the pleasure of interviewing the father in the hope that he could encourage Sam to change his ways. I read out some impressive test statistics concerning Sam's ability level and also tried to point out the benefits of qualifications to broaden his choices when he left school etc.

Throughout this speech, Sam's father looked almost asleep and as I wound up my carefully prepared plea he yawned and pronounced, 'Right chief. I know you mean well, but like Sam I don't believe school does any good! Look at me, I don't speak any languages, can hardly read, but I probably earn twice as much as you! The sooner he gets to work the better! Oh and by the way he won't be in school tomorrow 'cos we're short at the garage and he's good at changing tyres; and don't bother to check up because I can smell an attendance officer from a mile away and he'll be off like a shot!'

It was against this background that I watched Sam swagger across the playground with a certain amount of trepidation. Would it be another day of difficult decisions and disrupted lessons? Would I miss break again? And it was Friday, almond croissants and all!

He was three-quarters of the way across and his thoughts also seemed to be on food as he was striding purposefully towards the canteen. A teacher was behind me at the staffroom window and made a comment along the lines of 'Oh, the nutter's in, have a nice day Fozzie!' at which point Sam stopped, looked up and despite my attempt to duck below the window spotted me and my laughing colleague. He must have heard the comment as he poked his tongue out in our direction and treated us to a brief 'semi-moonie',(i.e. a bum shake with trousers still on) before continuing into the dining hall.

I watched for a few more minutes, fully expecting further developments, before settling with relief into my favourite armchair to sup on my customary coffee before the first lesson. A few minutes passed and then the staffroom phone rang ominously. It was too early for parental complaints and too late for the few sick teachers who were phoning in, so my fears were awakened. The teacher who was answering the phone had a serious look on his face and was scanning the room, eventually stopping at yours truly and pronouncing, 'There's trouble in the kitchen with Sam, could you go and help?'

Five minutes later I was faced with an unusual scene at the early morning food queue. This generally moved along quite quickly as only about ten or eleven pupils would be present at any time, unlike the traffic jam of lunch! But for some reason there was a line of about seven boys and girls behind Sam, a few looking quite disgruntled with the hold-up, which I couldn't explain at first glance as no one was being served and yet the dinner ladies were all in position, bacon at the ready! Sam was looking very stern-faced.

I decided to gather some information rather than jumping in at the deep end, so approached 'Gordon Ramsay' (my totally inappropriate nickname for the head of catering as he never swore) who informed me that Sam was trying to bypass the 'must carry a tray before collecting food' rule as he only wanted a bacon sandwich and 'was going to eat it outside, anyway!'

(also not allowed due to an increase in litter). I approached Sam in diplomatic mode and asked him if he would mind explaining the problem to me allowing the others in the queue to get their breakfast. He thought about this for a few moments before stating, 'But you won't let me go back to the front will you! I know where I was, it's in front of that ugly girl in my year.' As a tray slammed to the floor and the girl was approaching rapidly with a fist raised I realised that my diplomatic skills had failed and that we were now on 'war alert'. Whether Sam had engineered the situation by choosing a girl who was going through a bad acne phase is questionable, but I now needed to act quickly and put into place some of my boxing skills which had been acquired during a brief but interesting ten-week visit to our local gym at the age of fifteen (which I quite enjoyed until someone hit me very hard, an aspect of the sport that I should have given greater consideration to before attempting to become the next Cassius Clay). I had developed a reputation as a smooth mover who lacked any sort of punching power, or to put it more simply as the coach pointed out, 'Peter, you float like a butterfly and sting like one!' I must reassure the reader that I had no intention of hitting anyone, but hoped to use some nimble footwork to block any punches coming from either of the protagonists. My first move was excellent as a right hook in the general direction of Sam's chin was held at the last moment as I slid in expertly between the two of them. Unfortunately, I missed a grab for the girl's arm and there followed a period of 'manoeuvring for position', which even drew a small round of applause from the audience, who by this time had become far more interested in this contest than any thoughts of food. A second or so later I had managed to grab a left arm, but at the same time having moved to the side opened up the space for another right hook. The girl, like a true professional saw the gap and unleashed a real haymaker at Sam. Seeing the danger too late I moved back across between the two but was too slow and received the full force on my nose.

The blood spurted almost immediately, the girl was distraught trying to explain to all present that the punch had been intended for Sam ... and Sam had walked away laughing his head off!

I was shaken but not concussed and quickly applied the paper towel supplied by Gordon to my nose, which felt mushy but not completely ruined. The girl was by now in tears so after taking a seat I reassured her that I knew it was not deliberate, but needed to have a chat later about how to handle provocation. She went over to her friends who were trying to balance admiration for the quality of the punch with apparent concern for me. I had, of course, to consider what to do with Sam, but first needed to clean up before the pleasures of 2C history. I crossed the playground and realised that news on the school grapevine about the incident had somehow already reached the staffroom as a number of teachers were hanging out of the staffroom window and looking in my direction. I gave a brave thumbs-up and headed quickly for the men's loo where the mirror revealed that apart from some bruising, my beauty was still intact.

A number of my concerned teacher friends gave me some further checks and as I bravely left the staff-room there was the inevitable 'good left hook Harry' from someone, but apart from some questions and stares from 2C, the next hour or so was so quiet that I wondered if Sam had given up his quest for 'freedom' for at least that week.

I sent a written report of the incident to the headmaster and visited him at breaktime to discuss what to do with Sam etc. Thinking I had a broken nose, he asked me if I wanted to go home. I didn't overplay the situation, but got some brownie points by saying that although it was difficult to breathe I would prefer to stay and go for a check-up after school. He thought it best to take Sam out of classes to avoid further disruption, but it seems that as the rota system produced a teacher that regularly gave him 'grief' he decided to go home instead!

At least I could now settle down to lunch (Friday ... fish and chips + apple crumble ... yippee!) and start to contemplate a relaxing weekend.

Sam had, however, returned to school that afternoon, complaining of boredom as his dad had no work in the garage and decided to have one last crack at being expelled during lesson eight. On this occasion, in response to a perfectly reasonable request from a female teacher to stop making paper aeroplanes and sending them on test flights he produced 'the full moonie' for her pleasure and left us with no choice but to permanently exclude him.

We expected some sort of problem at the moment he was informed of this in the head's office, but he gracefully shook hands with the three teachers present and left with the remark, 'Don't worry, you're all OK. Thanks for trying with me ... I just can't stand school! If you need a car from my dad I'll do you a good deal!'

Although by this stage, Sam had become unteachable, this was only because he was on a mission to be expelled. I have only come across this once or twice during my career and the same can be said for a pupil who is completely out of control.

One of these latter rare occasions did occur on my first day at my third secondary school, a lovely building in the leafy London suburb of Bromley, where I had just been appointed head of P.E.

I was actually quite surprised to get this position, having tried unsuccessfully for about five 'second in department' positions over the previous few months. Some of these failures had left me a little downhearted as I had clearly thought myself to be the strongest candidate on at least two occasions and also believed I had given pretty solid interviews. So I had applied for this position more in hope than expectation, with the added incentive that the school was only a few miles from where I lived. I thus found myself in quite a relaxed mood as I looked around a waiting room containing seven other candidates, at least three of whom looked like the sort of elite sportsman that I wasn't. My sense of low expectation was further compounded by the fellow I was sitting next to who for some reason decided to not only tell me that he felt overqualified for the position, but also what he would do to 'shake things up' if he did decide to accept the position! Perhaps he was trying to psyche everyone else out before they went in to the interview. Anyway, my turn came and I gave relaxed and friendly answers to a series of fair questions, but felt that I had probably not come over as super-dynamic, or world changing, which was probably the result of suffering a series of previously stressful and more demanding interviews recently. I decided to read the staffroom newspaper when in came the headmaster's secretary to ask me to return to the interview room. Had I run over the school cat on my way in, or written something untruthful on my application ... or worse still was I the first to receive the dreaded 'debrief' as to why I hadn't 'been selected'? The headmaster's smiling face made me wonder for a moment and to my surprise a few moments later I was offered the post, which I accepted with a combination of pleasure and surprise.

And so here I was on my first day, feeling pretty pleased with things as the two lessons I had taught had both gone really well and the pupils and staff seemed to be friendly, one or two of the latter going out of their way to show me around and introduce me to the other teachers etc.

It seemed a really civilised place, a bit of a throwback to bygone days with good relationships between teachers and pupils. I had done well! My thoughts were drifting towards breaktime and how I would get a drink when a prefect came in and asked me if I would like a cup of tea from the canteen and a slice of today's 'special' fudge cake. I actually wanted to meet more of the staff, but he assured me that it was quite common for P.E. teachers to have this little traditional treat while the boys were changing, thus leaving time to still go to the staffroom at breaktime. So I gratefully accepted this offering. The fudge cake was very good and boded well for some yummy school grub at lunchtime. I was about to put my cup down, when one of the class I had just taken very politely offered to take it and my empty plate back to the canteen.

I was naturally further impressed by this attitude from a pupil and handed Danny my cup and plate. He looked at them both for a moment, seemingly comparing the two objects in some way, before placing the plate on a window sill. I suddenly realised that the whole changing room had gone quiet, but before I had a chance to work out why, a boy by a window had dived to his left as the cup flew past his right ear. The cup shattered the window and as I turned towards Danny he was taking aim with the plate (frisbee style) at the same boy. I just managed to grab his arm in time and the plate fell to the floor. Danny shouted, 'I'll have you later' towards his intended victim before running out of the changing room. One of the bolder pupils turned to me and said, 'Sir it's probably best not to provide Danny with any dangerous weapons; didn't anyone tell you about him?' There was a little laughter in the room and one or two smirks that I interpreted as being something like 'the new teacher's a bit green'. My authority was being challenged! Should I deal with Danny later or show the lads what I was made of? I decided on the latter course of action and after issuing an instruction to the prefect to not let the class leave until the bell, I set off in pursuit of Danny.

He was at the end of a rather grand corridor (a remnant of the school's former life as a manor house) and as a number of staff and pupils were at various points in the corridor, I decided not to lose face by breaking in to a run and instead issued an authoritative, 'Danny, wait right there!' to which he responded with two fingers planted firmly into the air. He didn't, however realise that the headmaster was right behind him and almost bumped into him as he turned to run.

Realising that two escape routes were blocked, he shot off down another corridor in one last bid for freedom, only to be knocked flat by a door opened by one of the school secretaries coming out of her office. (There followed a two-week debate in the staffroom about whether this normally very mild mannered lady had done this deliberately or not.) As if by magic, two other teachers appeared and proceeded to sit on Danny whilst the headmaster issued an order for him to calm down if he wanted them to get off. A few seconds of struggle ensued but as I finally reached the scene of the action, Danny had agreed to come into the headmaster's office. I was also asked to come in to give an account of the incident, which took me about three minutes. During this 'report', Danny was looking surly and slightly threatening and he also told us that the boy who he had aimed the cup at had 'given him a dirty look' earlier in the day. This was obviously a pretty flimsy defence and he couldn't really include me as a reason for his loss of temper as we had no history, with it being my first day. At the end of this 'trial', the head announced the inevitable news that he was to receive three strikes of the cane and proceeded to pick up a long willowy stick just behind him and said, 'Right, over to the chair' which was used as a sort of steadying place with the victim gripping the top of the backrest. Danny had other ideas, however, and after pronouncing 'No way!' he looked quickly round the room and then ran over to an open window which he vaulted very neatly and then broke into a steady run out of the school gates, never to be seen again, despite many attempts from the school and Education Authority to force him to return.

I found out subsequently that despite a great deal of 'missionary zeal' Danny was not only practically unteachable, but also a potential danger to both pupil and teacher. As is often the case with severely disruptive students, his family background was both violent and uncaring.

Occasionally, two children from the same family are complete opposites with regard to behaviour. In some cases the reasons are clear, such as one being the praised favourite and the other being treated as not being as good in so many ways that they believe it themselves, or they simply decide to behave badly to attract attention. It is always more surprising when the family is equally as caring and supportive to both children and yet their offspring are clearly as different as chalk and cheese.

Take Jane and William, for example. Jane was the perfect student. Top sets for every subject; a prime candidate for head girl, and a delight to teach. It would have been so easy to have speeded up every lesson by just letting her answer every time a question was aired to the class, but, of course, teachers must be fair to everyone!

She also had a lovely personality, with a great sense of humour and winning smile to boot.

William by contrast was older by a year and a real tearaway. He had been excluded a number of times, was often involved in fights with other pupils and verbal confrontation with teachers.

His parents and sister attempted to be very supportive towards him, but he resented her, possibly feeling academically inferior, although everyone was very careful not to confront him with his sister's success story in comparison with his wild behaviour.

Jane went to university and William faced an uncertain future after permanent exclusion!

I'll end this chapter with one of my favourite history classes.

The lesson on World War One had been well prepared and the previous lead-up work had left the class waiting eagerly to find out more about the suffering in the trenches. I had created a 'night time in the trenches' soundtrack as an opening activity, and had decided to ask the boys and girls to just sit down, close their eyes and then try to work out what was going on and how it made them feel. Just in case someone opened their eyes, I had also blacked out the room with blinds down and lights off.

As they listened, my eyes wandered round the group in the gloom and I began to reflect on why this was my favourite class.

It was a mixed ability group, which made life a little bit more difficult for me as I needed to differentiate the work to a certain extent; and they were also a mixture of personalities ... Jimmy in the corner would never speak up or offer an answer, unless asked to, but Rachel had to be restrained from trying to answer everything. There were pupils with a wide range of ability and differing personalities, and yet they were as a unit perfectly well behaved. Did I like them so much because they were so well behaved?

I occasionally taught a class of high-ability, but really boring, individuals who on paper outshone this present group. My attempts to vary the lesson content and methods were often met by incredulous stares from a group who only seemed happy when writing down some 'concrete detail', or working silently copying a series of facts. Even tests were popular as it was an environment for silent work.

No, it wasn't just that they were also well behaved. There were, despite their differences, just so many great young people in the group. They also respected each other (and the teacher I believe) and this all added up to a relaxed, yet exciting, environment. It was as if I was on a visit to an interesting historical building or landmark with a group of friends who shared my interest.

It's classes like this that make teaching such a rewarding profession.

Marking can be fun

Actually, it's far from fun most of the time, a fact I won't have to tell thousands of teachers!

The idea that a teacher's day is actually quite short is, of course, a myth. Good lessons rarely just happen, although there are a number of geniuses in the teaching profession who can not only think on their feet but also have such a grasp of their subject that they can sometimes deliver an excellent lesson 'off the cuff'. This is rare, however as even the best lesson plan needs updating each year and almost inevitably, modifying, for a group with a different ability level etc.

And marking is another huge burden of extra time. I have always admired the teachers who stay behind each day to not only prepare future lessons, but to complete all their marking. I always found this a difficult idea with freedom beckoning and preferred to mark at home, but this was sometimes not a good plan either as I could easily delay the start of my marking session at least once or twice by convincing myself that I needed a rest after such a strenuous day!

Being a P.E. and history teacher I was actually quite lucky with my marking workload and in a typical week found myself facing about six sets of exercise books, compared with the ten or more that most poor teachers faced.

No, I am not suggesting that the grinding routine of marking is anything less than hard and often boring, but there are moments when marking can be genuinely funny...

One bright summer's day I took my seat in the staff-room and proceeded to sup my lunchtime coffee. An English teacher sat down next to me and gradually drew my attention as she was purring about the quality of the English homework she was marking. I wasn't surprised when I noticed her giving Jane and Chris high marks as I recognised them as good pupils, but I did notice that she seemed to be marking very quickly and constantly checking the clock. At one point she said, 'I forgot to take these home last night and I've got the class in thirty minutes, so I have to finish the marking.' A phone call further reduced her available time so much that she was really rushing through the pages of the last few exercise books with only a few minutes of lunchtime left.

I glanced over again and noticed she was marking the notorious Sam's homework (a wild spirit determined to be expelled ... sorry, permanently excluded) and was surprised to note that he had received an A for 'What I did last weekend'. It was unusual for our young rebel to even bother to do his homework, let alone achieve a high mark, so I asked if I could have a read. Sam was capable of neat writing when motivated, but this seemed excessively neat and careful at first glance and I was further surprised to note that he had completed three sides of foolscap. Did this teacher have the answer to getting Sam to behave and work?

I started to read and within a few lines his intentions were revealed. Rather than describe some tinkering with a car engine or a day out with his mates, he had described in graphic, no holds barred, detail what he and his girlfriend had got up to in his room while his parents were out. I must admit to blushing at some of the descriptive work and the final insult was at the end where there was a detailed comparison of his girlfriend's good looks with a number of 'not as fit' female teachers.

I found myself giggling as this normally very thorough teacher had been so pushed for marking time that she had just glanced at the very neat writing and impressive length of the essay and awarded not only a top mark but the unfortunate comment, 'Keep up the good work at home!'

I promised not to tell anyone and we shared a laugh after the teacher had got over her initial embarrassment. It was also possible to rub out her pencil marks and comments to save further blushes.

Marking tests can also occasionally be cause for mirth as the following answers to history test questions clearly demonstrate...

Question: 'What was the purpose of the trenches built in the First World War?'
Answer: 'The soldiers grew vegetables in them.'

Question: 'Who was shot in Sarajevo to spark the beginning of World War One?'
Answer: 'Rio Ferdinand.'

(I rather harshly decided this didn't deserve even a half point as the correct answer was Arch Duke Ferdinand.)

Question: 'What were early medieval sailors worried about when they sailed west from Europe?'
Answer: 'The USA'

Question: 'What were the ladies who fought for the right to vote called?'
Answer: 'I don't know and I'm bored with this test.'

Marking can also be fun when the work is so good that it takes over your attention in the way that a good book, or an interesting discussion can sometimes do.

I recall one such evening when after a difficult day at school I forced myself to mark a set of history home-works that needed to be completed before the next lesson only a couple of days away.

Although 'not in the mood' I did have reasonable expectations for the classes' efforts, as the homework project was the end result of a series of really enjoyable lessons on the slave trade where I had managed to combine some real life accounts with some drama work and also some selected sections from Stephen Spielberg's excellent film *Amistad*.

The pupils' brief was to imagine they were a slave and write a diary of their experiences. They were also encouraged to be creative about presentation by using 'ageing' methods on their chosen paper such as soaking in tea, wrinkling of paper and burning edges (health and safety emphasised here of course) and to include some drawings or pictures to illustrate their work.

The diaries had to have at least four entries, including an outline of their life in Africa and descriptions of home and family, the day of capture, the journey across the Atlantic in a slave ship, and a description of a day of their new life on a cotton or sugar plantation.

On flicking through the papers in front of me I realised almost immediately that nearly everyone had done more than the minimum.

Sitting next to me was my wife, one of my daughters and my grandson, who would have been about nine at the time. In front of us on the telly was a rather second-rate science fiction film, which, nevertheless, had received the majority vote for the evening's activities. (My grandson had voted for Monopoly, but as I had received a good thrashing from him the previous evening courtesy of some very unlucky rolls of the dice that landed me on his Mayfair, complete with hotel, three circuits in a row, I was keen to squash this idea, which would have also taken me away from the marking.)

I was tempted to start by marking one the best pupil's work, but decided to save this till later in case I needed a 'lift' and thus decided to take them in the order they were stacked.

Imagine my surprise when marking one of the laziest members of the class's work and finding not only a beautifully presented project, but one full of excellent detail and imagination. I gave this a high mark and moved on to the next document. My surprise this time was firstly that this pupil (a regular homework 'refuser') had even bothered with the task and secondly that the work was of a standard hitherto never seen from this individual!

And on and on went the happy story ... I realised after about five pieces of work that the subject must have really interested the students and that I could hardly wait to turn a page for the next bit of the story.

As I completed marking a book I placed it on the floor and the rest of my family started to read and make suggestions as to an acceptable mark for each piece of work.

After about fifteen minutes we all agreed to turn off the telly and for the next hour and a half we were all totally engrossed by slave diaries.

There followed a final ordering of the work from best to worst and a discussion on which pieces of work deserved to receive a credit, or even better a recommendation to be viewed by the headmaster. By bedtime the whole family had had an enjoyable and informative few hours!

I returned all of the work at the end of the school year, but managed to track down one former pupil, Becky, who kindly agreed to allow me to show some of her original pages in this book.

The first few pages are selections from her slave diary and then I have included some extracts from her equally good work based on Anne Frank, where the class were asked to imagine themselves in her situation and write some diary entries to an imaginary friend. Once again, the quality and amount of work from nearly all the pupils was excellent. Being year eight and roughly the same age as Anne when she went into hiding made it all the more relevant and poignant, and an excellent BBC documentary on Anne provided further moving detail and visual stimulus.

Becky, it was always a pleasure to teach you and I even enjoyed marking your work!!!

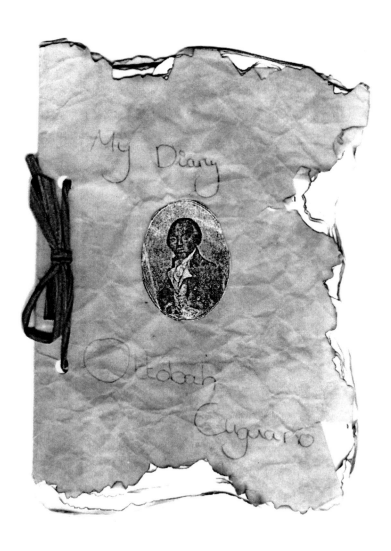

Dear diary,

My name is Ottobah Cuguano; I live with my family in Benin. In Benin the weather here is usually hot and the temperature is around 24° and 31°C. My family and I work as farmers, our two children work on one of the farms a few miles from here. We get up at 4:00am and it is straight to work, we don't get paid that much but what ever we do get paid it goes straight towards a better life. We live in a small hut. It is very small there and quite cramped, but it is sometimes cosy.

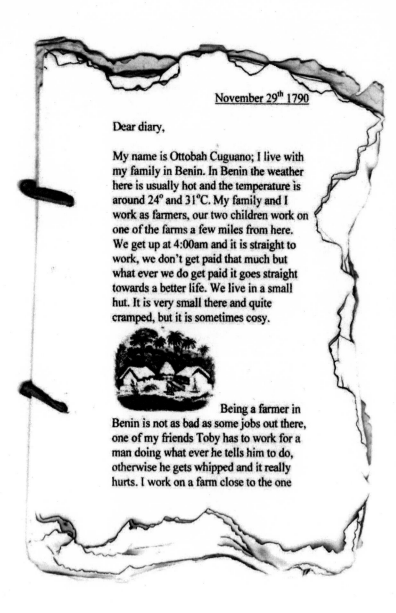

Being a farmer in Benin is not as bad as some jobs out there, one of my friends Toby has to work for a man doing what ever he tells him to do, otherwise he gets whipped and it really hurts. I work on a farm close to the one

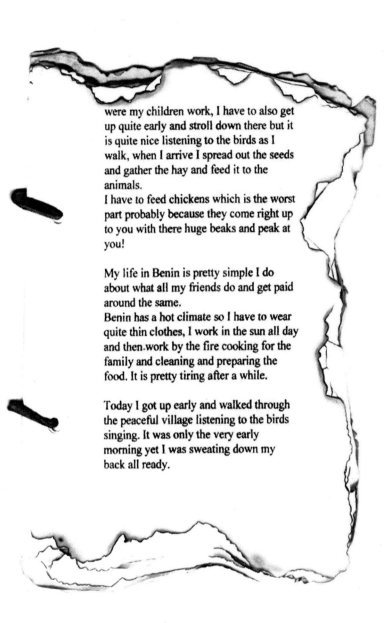

were my children work, I have to also get
up quite early and stroll down there but it
is quite nice listening to the birds as I
walk, when I arrive I spread out the seeds
and gather the hay and feed it to the
animals.
I have to feed chickens which is the worst
part probably because they come right up
to you with there huge beaks and peak at
you!

My life in Benin is pretty simple I do
about what all my friends do and get paid
around the same.
Benin has a hot climate so I have to wear
quite thin clothes, I work in the sun all day
and then work by the fire cooking for the
family and cleaning and preparing the
food. It is pretty tiring after a while.

Today I got up early and walked through
the peaceful village listening to the birds
singing. It was only the very early
morning yet I was sweating down my
back all ready.

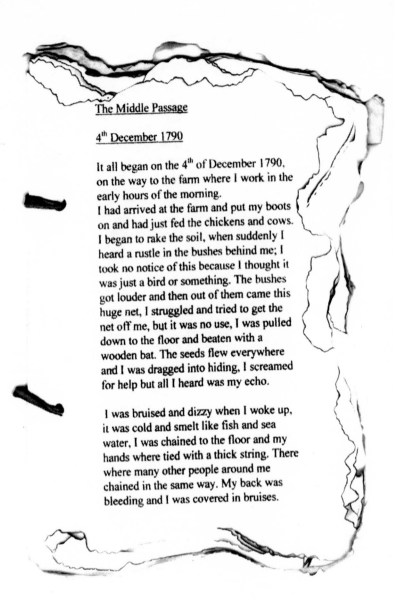

The Middle Passage

4th December 1790

It all began on the 4th of December 1790, on the way to the farm where I work in the early hours of the morning.
I had arrived at the farm and put my boots on and had just fed the chickens and cows. I began to rake the soil, when suddenly I heard a rustle in the bushes behind me; I took no notice of this because I thought it was just a bird or something. The bushes got louder and then out of them came this huge net, I struggled and tried to get the net off me, but it was no use, I was pulled down to the floor and beaten with a wooden bat. The seeds flew everywhere and I was dragged into hiding, I screamed for help but all I heard was my echo.

I was bruised and dizzy when I woke up, it was cold and smelt like fish and sea water, I was chained to the floor and my hands where tied with a thick string. There where many other people around me chained in the same way. My back was bleeding and I was covered in bruises.

Freedom

Today is the day; I have been counting down the days, the weeks and the months. I was going to escape while Mr Giggs went of to the auction once again, I was left to clean, wash the clothes and prepare for lunch, but not as far as I was concerned. I was going to make a great escape that would go down in history as the man who escaped from his terrifying owner; I could see it right now. I was going to creep out the barn and squeeze through the gap in the gate and steal one of those horses that I would clean up after everyday and ride away in disguise, I already took some of Mr Giggs clothes and covered them up with hay in the barn ready for today.

Mr Giggs came into my barn and I was shovelling horse manure into a sack, he told me that I was to get on with what I had to do and he would deal with me when he came back. He shut the door and went away. I waited a few minutes, I shot of and ran as fast as I could in Mr Giggs clothes I jumped on the horse and rode away I couldn't believe I was out of this.

My
Diary
by
Rebekah

<u>Sunday, 5 July 1942</u>

Dear diary,

Today father sat me and mother down, he never usually dose this so it must have been important.

He began by informing us that we were going to go in hiding (I distinctively remember the word "hiding" because as he said it he looked down and a small tear trickled down his pale face.)

He told us that the Nazi party were coming for German Jews.

So that was that next week we
would be moving into our secret
hiding place, he told us that it was
above his office and that we had to
be very discrete about where, when
and who was moving into this secret
annex.

I have decided to confide
everything to you, as I have never
been capable to confide in anyone.
In order to confide in you I
think you deserve a name so I will
call you Honeychild.

Someone is calling me.

Yours Rebekah

<u>*Wednesday 28 January 1943*</u>

Dearest Honeychild,

As the New Year has approached it is just a little while longer until we will be free.

It is my favourite time of the year, winter. I enjoy this time because I like the regular snow here and the mixed emotions my window friend have towards the snow, many enjoy throwing the snow at each other, while some people who over the weeks of sitting here I have learnt that they dislike the idea of snow touching there pale faces and building snow men, and prefer sitting in a warm house by the fire drinking hot coco.

The majority of children my age like playing with their friends shooting snow at one another. However the young ones cry if snow even comes remotely close to them, the elderly just walk on by dodging the snow coming at them. All I want on the world right now is what most of my window friends take for granted, freedom.

Time to say goodbye

As the teacher stood up I had a tightening in my stomach muscles. He was looking the worst for wear due to a few too many drinks at the end of year party and there was a general feeling amongst the staff that he had not received the promotions he had deserved during his years at the school. Was this the moment for revenge?

He slowly took out some notes from his pocket, smiled momentarily on recognising the contents and then made a few pointed stares at certain teachers. A wobble suggested that he might topple over and save all present from the barbed comments that we all expected, but he recovered quickly and with a hitch of the trousers and a deep breath began his speech.

I had better leave the actual detail of this speech out!!

Fortunately, a vitriolic leaving speech is the exception rather than the rule. I have witnessed some really funny people make us all laugh our socks off at stories about strange pupils who did this or that, or the members of their departments with amusing characteristics etc. If that member of staff has been very popular and also long-serving, then a good, funny speech is almost a relief as it holds back the tears and emotion for at least a few minutes.

There are also the speeches where emotion takes over completely and a normally lucid teacher is reduced to a blubbering wreck, usually at the mention of the first of their really close friends.

'I won't make a long speech, but I can't leave without thanking certain people,' were the only words managed by one 'blubberer' before she made the mistake of meeting the tear-filled eyes of her best friend. A potentially awkward moment was averted by three of her other friends rushing up to give her a hug, plus a good round of applause from the assembled masses.

The worst leaving speech I ever heard was about fifteen sides of foolscap detailing not just the individual's teaching career, but also practically his whole life from infant school upwards. This was delivered in a monotone, which further added to the general sense of tedium. A number of teachers left before the end and the headteacher mercifully interrupted proceedings after about 20 minutes.

I also found it quite emotional when pupils left, either at the end of year eleven or to university at the end of the sixth form. Everyone has their favourites and after teaching students for five or more years it is only natural to feel that you have seen and been a part of their journey towards adulthood. Most of the spotty little 'oiks' I first met in year seven have developed into delightful and talented young ladies and gentlemen. Even some of the less popular members of a year often surprise you when they leave. 'I'm sorry I was such a pain in your lesson Sir, I actually wish I could start again and get some decent exam results; anyway, thanks for trying!' was about the nicest thing one particular boy ever said to me, it's just a pity that his 'conversion' was on the day he left.

In fact, when I meet former pupils outside school they are also nearly always very pleasant. Only a few weeks ago I had only just settled into my seat on a bus when a particularly muscular (very badly behaved) former pupil jumped on at the next stop. What would I do if he swore at, or even threatened, me? A look around the bus confirmed that it was quite full and it was too late to bury my face in the newspaper I had been reading. Also, if I hid my face I might have missed any punch coming my way. I wished I hadn't given him all those detentions!

Having decided I had no option but to await my fate, I smiled briefly at him and proceeded to pretend to take in the scenery. To my horror he slipped smoothly into the seat right next to me!

'Hi Mr Fos, I expect I'm the last person you want to see! Well, I've got a surprise for you. I didn't end up in prison and I did decide to take the plumbing course the careers lady told me was just right for me. I passed it, worked for a friend for three years and now I've opened up my own business with two other blokes working for me. I also married Katie, you know, the good-looking blonde I was always dodging lessons with and we're looking for our own place as the business is doing so well!' He then slapped me on the shoulder, said I was an 'all right' teacher and left at the next stop.Occasionally I am reminded of my advancing years by former pupils. At a recent prize-giving ceremony a fifty-year old gentleman came up to me, shook hands and then launched into some ancient stories about school football teams and great goals etc.

I actually didn't have a clue who he was until he reminded me that I substituted him in the district cup final, only for his replacement to score an own goal. Before he left he hammered in the age 'nail' even further by reminding me that his daughter had also been to and left the school!

The final day of school for year eleven pupils was always a fun affair! They were allowed to leave early after a final year assembly where form tutors and year heads would receive a 'thank you' and present, but this was always a bit of an anti-climax and it was often pre-ceded and followed by groups of boys and girls roaming round the school trying to say goodbye to their favourite teachers in the middle of other lessons. A messy state of affairs further compounded by the traditional 'fancy dress' worn by the boys and girls, which was a long way from standard school uniform! This could be anything at all for the boys; on my last year eleven leaving day we had Superman, Batman and Robin, a Sumo wrestler bouncing off everyone and everything and a number of boys who cross-dressed. The tradi-tional girls' gear was short skirts with fishnet tights and lashings of lipstick and other make-up.

It was also the norm to sign each other's shirts with some sort of leaving message. Although the occasional 'I hate you' appeared on one or two shirts, I must say that the general level of comments were very pleasant and certainly added some colour to the occasion.

The day was, however, becoming a difficult one. No one wanted to spoil the students' fun, but it was difficult to manage the rest of the school with all the high jinks going on.

Then one of the year heads had a brainwave. Her idea was to have a full-blown party for the leavers in the main hall. They would only come into school at about 11a.m., have a brunch and some soft drinks and then be entertained by volunteers who wished to sing, dance or entertain the audience with some witty stories about school etc. They would then leave school at about 1.30p.m. with a posse of teachers cheerfully waving them goodbye on a carefully selected route off the site. In addition a small number who had behaved badly in the lead up to the final day would be banned from the event.

This format worked really well from the outset. Even the small minority who felt they should have been allowed to bring alcohol conceded that as they were leaving school so early, there would be plenty of time for a 'real' party in the evening.

I still, however, had a feeling that the leaving 'experience' was missing something and then I remembered that many years ago we used to produce a school yearbook. Why not re-introduce this for year eleven only each year as a memory of their school career, something they would re-open in later years and share with their family? In 2000 I also had an additional personal interest as I was head of year eleven, so I sat down with a volunteer group of about ten to discuss both the format of the book and who would take on which task etc. We had also contacted two or three yearbook companies and had examples of their work to inspire us!

There was a surprising amount of agreement about some of the pages, with student and teacher photo collages coming top, closely followed by a message page where everyone could write their thank yous and good-byes. An original addition to the photo suggestion was a baby photo page, as everyone would have great fun working out who had grown up into who. A 'rate the teacher' page was discarded as being potentially too explosive, as was a 'get it off your chest' section which could have proved libellous.

By this time the team of ten had been reduced to a 'magnificent seven' (as three only joined in the hope that they would be missing a number of lessons), who eventually produced the first of a number of yearbooks. We managed to get some sponsorship from one or two local firms as well as a kind grant from the school and this brought the cost down to such a reasonable level that we managed to sell copies to over half the year group and about fifteen teachers closely connected to the pupils concerned.

In the following years even more were sold, and as rising costs became an issue and technology improved, the school eventually took over the complete production process, which introduced yet another element, a computer team beavering away at lunchtime and after school.

On the next few pages are some examples of a typical yearbook.

As my last few months before retirement approached I decided to plan an event to say thank you to all my teaching friends over the years.

Despite the vagaries of the British summer, I decided to have a barbecue in our reasonable-sized garden a week or so before the end of term. My family were keen to help, with the biggest burden falling on my wife, who agreed to organise and prepare the food.

Some friends offered a marquee for the occasion, which just about fitted on our lawn and was large enough to be insurance against rain. It was quite a heavy package to lump in the car, but the collection went without a hitch, apart from me picking up a speeding fine on the way back. (I thought that for 36mph in a 30 area it was a little harsh!)

Nearly all my friends and family turned up and we all had a lovely (dry and warm) evening with music supplied by Mike and a wonderful spread of food supplied by my wife. The neighbours had also been invited as a sort of thank you for putting up with a potentially noisy evening and on the accommodation front, the summer house we had built a few years before served very well as an extra seating area.

It was quite emotional for me to say goodbye to so many old friends, but I tried to hold myself together as I was also the host. I was assisted in this respect by one or two close friends who, knowing that I could easily become the worse for wear after only a couple of lagers, proceeded to continually replenish my glass with a non-alcoholic variety of 'Euro fizz', but as the party approached a late hour, I had to suddenly put my thinking cap on as Mike had brought a lump to my throat with a short but very complementary speech about not only my teaching career and friendship, but also what a great evening it had been.

I had to respond, which I believe I did quite adequately and also managed to include a big thank you to everyone who had helped with the party, especially my wife, without whom the event most certainly would not have been such a success.

If I had drunk some real lager I would have followed this short speech up with Elvis' 'The Wonder of You' in honour of my wife, but as applause burst out I satisfied myself with a purposeful stride towards my adoring fans for a few farewell hugs and kisses ... except I had forgotten I was two steps up on the summer house patio!

As I crashed into the throng below, I realised in a split second that I was heading straight for the three-year-old son of a friend, who up to that moment had been enjoying a fun evening of food and outdoor games!

Despite my best efforts I landed on top of him, but was relieved to find that he was not only alive, but unhurt and to his credit, not really crying.

With the realisation that all was well, the joke was very much on me and I was even allowed to have an alcoholic drink, provided I took any step one at a time!

And so my final day arrived. It would of course end in a local pub towards the evening, but during the day I tried to get round the school to say a fond goodbye to all my favourite pupils and teachers.

At the end of term barbecue it was traditional to have a few drinks and some food as people arrived at different times, but the leaving speeches were soon on the agenda.

As the longest-serving teacher I had expected to be the last to speak but was called on first, after three of my colleagues had 'introduced' me with some stories about me from the near and distant past.

I had determined not to waffle on for too long or repeat a much-heard old story (both common faults of mine) and concentrate on a brief résumé of my career with some humour and thank yous thrown in along the way.

As I opened my mouth I hoped that I wouldn't become one of the blubber brigade, or fall over again!

My only real blunder was to turn over two pages instead of one of my cue cards towards the end of the speech, thus forgetting to thank my good friend Steve for coming all the way from Scotland for my leaving do (and a few days golf), or mention a long serving secretary at the school who I had only just discovered was at the same primary school as me 50 years earlier. (Was she the good looker in the year above who I had a bit of a crush on?)

I was helped by some good recent material provided not only by teachers, but also my last form group who gave me a lovely leaving present and a touching and funny leaving card, which included the following comments;

'Don't worry, just because you're sixty doesn't mean you are going to lose your libido!'

'I suggest you use your pension to buy drugs as you'll have plenty of time to relax.'

'Thanks for being a great form tutor and for trying to make a funny joke for five years!'

I woke the next day to the prospect of retirement ... a new phase of my life which I am enjoying tremendously, with so much more time for my hobbies and family etc.

This book started in the 1970s, when I began jotting down some funny moments in my teaching life. I am not sure if I had any clear ideas about a book at the time. As the years went on I continued to scribble down bits and pieces right up to 2008 when I retired, and also collect material from pupils and the schools I have worked in. It has taken quite a while to sift through some of the good or bad bits and there was also a delay due to a move of house to deepest Kent and the inevitable subsequent decorating etc.

I hope that my friends have enjoyed these memories and if anyone from a wider audience should have ventured into the book that they have been entertained!

I must point out that the schools I have worked in are not the 'mad' places they may appear to be from my stories. For every strange or funny incident mentioned there were far more 'normal' working days!

Teaching can be a struggle at times, but as I think back over my career it brings mostly a smile to my face. Being in an environment where young people are developing and learning is exciting and rewarding, and often very funny. I have also worked with teachers whose ability to interest, inform, and create a 'fun' atmosphere has often been inspirational!

If anyone out there is thinking of becoming a teacher for the money (not a lot) or holidays, think again! But if you have a love of a subject or two plus a strong desire to work with young people, you might just be entering one of the most rewarding of professions.

Good luck!

About the author

Peter lives in Kent with his wife Francien. His three children and two grandchildren are not too far away in south east London.

His interests include drawing, reading and visiting historical sites.

On the sporting front, he is still trying to improve his golf swing and enjoys hiking and fishing in The Weald and beyond.